dear Carol

your friendship is precious to me. your story could easily be written in this book.

Hope your day is special

love
De Ann
1977

Love Is the Gift

Love Is
the Gift

AFTON GRANT AFFLECK

BOOKCRAFT, INC.
Salt Lake City, Utah

Library of Congress Catalog Card Number: 77-75305
ISBN 0-88494-316-X

2nd Printing, 1977

Lithographed in the United States of America
PUBLISHERS PRESS
Salt Lake City, Utah

To Charlie Stewart
whose life taught me much about the power of
love and who on his deathbed committed me to
the struggle and the joy of writing this book

Contents

Our Panoramic Vision

Preface

This book will confirm the testimony of those who know, with John, that "every one that loveth is born of God." The true accounts it contains demonstrate the power of love in action — in service to our spirit brothers and sisters. Deliberately they have been selected to indicate the range of possible service, from the "ordinary" family situation to the so-called hardened criminal. They demonstrate that no one's personal problem is beyond the reach of service given in love, the service that Jesus exemplifies.

I express appreciation to all those who have generously shared their experiences for inclusion in this book and have agreed that names of givers and receivers should be changed in order to protect privacy and to reflect the purity of purpose in bestowing the gift of love. (Exceptions as regards change of name, made for obvious reasons, are chapters 17 and 23.)

My thanks go to Betty Jean Young and Sue Russell, who assisted with the typing; to Elaine Jack, Sally Black, and Elaine Smart, who from their vantage point gave splendid criticism and suggestions; and to Ranon Hulet, who encouraged me when I especially needed it. My heartfelt appreciation is extended also to Roseanna Moss, who in typing the last drafts of the manuscript became a trusted and wise counselor and friend.

I express deep appreciation and love to my husband Robert,

whose confidence in me gave me the much-needed encouragement to write the book; and to our children, Grant and Sonja,
Connie Jean and Pete, and Steven and Karin for being conscien-
tious reactors to the manuscript.

At the risk of being repetitious I acknowledge with deep
gratitude my debt to Charlie Stewart not only for his conceiving
the idea of the book but for just being the superb example he
was.

Finally, I seek to express the inexpressible — my profound
and fervent thanks to the Father of us all, together with my
totally inadequate praise for his gifts of love.

1 For Example

As the second advent of our Lord and Savior draws near, it becomes increasingly apparent that throughout the world there is emanating from the Spirit of the Lord an illumination of the need each of us has for the other. Many people are moving into areas of service, enlisting in the fight against sin and suffering.

As we move from "hearers of the word" to "doers," we glimpse a possible fusing of all men into the brotherhood the Savior envisioned when he said: "By this shall all men know that ye are my disciples, if ye have love one to another." (John 13:35.)

A young man of my acquaintance has developed a rare concept. He believes he should spend a good portion of his time and money helping others. This would not be rare except that in his case the giving spills over from his private life into his business life.

Jon has always been service-oriented. He learned to give as a child. Together his family would decide if someone in distress needed food, clothing, or other commodities. They would assemble the needed items and deliver them secretly in the night. The gifts were anonymous. They never spoke of them to anyone, not even to one another. Written on a paper taped to the window frame above the kitchen sink were the words of the Savior:

But when thou doest alms, let not thy left hand know what thy right hand doeth:

That thine alms may be in secret: and thy Father which seeth in secret himself shall reward thee openly. (Matthew 6:3-4.)

The family learned that when they gave, the Lord blessed them individually in the areas of their lives where they most needed a blessing. Jon relates that they also came to realize that being kind and thoughtful were rewarding gifts worthy of giving.

Jon's giving has magnified in scope. Many missionaries have been financially able to serve on missions because as an unknown benefactor Jon has deposited money in a bank in their names. Others are invited to go to designated department stores and select needed clothing.

Jon helps people pay delinquent accounts; then he assists them to set up realistic budgets. He spends hours counseling youth and adults, and he motivates them to realize that life is to be lived fully — that they have possibilities and potential unlimited. "Success and happiness don't just happen," Jon maintains. "You make them happen by living the law upon which the desired blessing is predicated." (See D&C 130:20-21.)

The successful corporation of which he is president has explored ways to serve the community. They desire to give service in areas that will not be construed as advertising or public relations schemes. They've found a need. They have a plan. They are moving forward. Exciting things are happening to Jon, the corporation, the personnel. Perhaps this is because he is following the pattern indicated by Jacob, a Book of Mormon prophet.

Think of your brethren like unto yourselves, and be familiar with all and free with your substance, that they may be rich like unto you.

But before ye seek for riches, seek ye for the kingdom of God.

And after ye have obtained a hope in Christ ye shall obtain riches, if ye seek them; and ye will seek them for the intent to do good — to clothe the naked, and to feed the hungry, and to liberate the captive, and administer relief to the sick and the afflicted. (Jacob 2:17-19.)

The extraordinary truth is that Jon is like the man in the verse:

> There was a man,
> Though some did think him mad,
> The more he gave away
> The more he had.

Money and material substance is only one way of giving. I have a "bubbly," enthusiastic friend. She values people. Her goal is to give love daily to at least one person. Her gift of love is listening.

She never lacks recipients — people are drawn to her. She says, "I fill myself up with love and listen — not for words, but for needs, for feelings, and for meanings." She never repeats to the speaker precisely what he has said, but she asks: "Is this how you feel? Is this what you mean?" She rarely gives advice or recites trite formulas that are presupposed cures.

"I never rob people of their burdens; I try to lend them strength to carry them. Listening does that. It clarifies thinking and eases heartache; then there can come new perspectives. Solutions come when someone listens — listens with the sincere concentration of love. Solutions revealed to us personally seem not only plausible but possible."

She reminds me that some people don't need someone to listen to their problems; their need is to share happiness, achievements, and new ideas and discoveries. "When you listen and rejoice, their new knowledge or experience becomes an integral part of them, claimed forever. That doesn't happen until one has the opportunity to share."

Her life is exciting and challenging. She is filled with constant wonder at the Lord's blessing her with daily opportunities to give her gift.

She "halves people's sorrows and doubles their joys."

I had occasion to drop in on a ward New Year's Eve party in a densely populated area of a city. My first reaction was surprise at the number of people in attendance, in view of the many sophisticated choices offered on New Year's Eve. I sensed a deep unity and oneness among the people — young and old. Just before midnight, all participated in a Grand March. Youth and adults saluted one another with smiles and nods. Joyfully, they marched together. A tiny youngster struggled to keep up. Occasionally someone would lean over, pick him up, and carry him a little way so that he could keep pace. The excitement of love and fellowship was electric.

After the Grand March I began to ask questions. It was then I learned about the service project called the "Twelve Days of Christmas."

The young people had asked the bishop's permission to make the legend of the "Twelve Days of Christmas" come alive. The plan was to divide among them the elderly people within the ward boundaries, both members and nonmembers, and give each a gift of service for the twelve days preceding Christmas.

The project gained momentum. Creativity reigned. The girls baked bread, cake, and cookies; and the boys made gifts, did simple household repairs, and shoveled snow. Those with drivers' licenses ran errands and took their special friends shopping. Together they wrapped gifts, washed windows, did ironing and mending, sang carols, and listened — relaxed and unhurried — to tales of "When I was young . . ." and "I remember when. . . ." Love and closeness grew between giver and receiver. The elderly felt renewed vigor through the joy of being loved, and served, and listened to.

As the second advent of our Lord and Savior draws near, it becomes increasingly apparent that throughout the world there is emanating from the Spirit of the Lord an illumination of the need each of us has for the other. Many people are moving into areas of service, enlisting in the fight against sin and suffering.

As we move from "hearers of the word" to "doers," we glimpse a possible fusing of all men into the brotherhood the Savior envisioned when he said: "By this shall all men know that ye are my disciples, if ye have love one to another." (John 13:35.)

At the time of writing, Belfast, Ireland, is divided into polarized areas, Protestant and Catholic settlements, each at war with the other. The city is torn with violence and hate. Families sit behind barred doors as TV screens spew venom. Children live with fear. They are acquainted with hate. They hurl bottles and stones at one another and run shrieking in the streets, waving wooden guns.

An unusual group of women, sickened with realization that these children are the men and women of tomorrow, began working together toward a new hope for peace.

It occurred to one caring woman that women of both sides must be brought together to work for peace. Church leaders felt this would not be possible; the situation was too delicate. The woman who cared felt that some of them would "have to be fools for the Savior's sake." She found fifteen women, Catholic and Protestant, who agreed that they rejected violence as a means for attaining any goal. They placed ads in Belfast newspapers, inviting all women who were opposed to violence and who wished to dedicate themselves to peace to meet together. Their purpose was to organize a Women Together movement in which women could become as actively involved and dedicated to peace as were those who were convinced that violence was the answer to social injustices. Buses would bring the women to the designated hall.

At the appointed time of eight o'clock, there were only six women in their seats. At 8:15 P.M., the doors flew open. Hundreds of women surged in. The buses had been tied up in traffic.

The goal was explained. There was a coolness, a mistrust and a mutual suspicion, until a woman from Catholic Falls stood. For a moment she hesitated. There was absolute silence, then she extended her arms and in a tremulous voice pleaded, "I want to shake hands with a woman from Protestant Shankill." The women arose as one, hands extended, and moved toward each other. That night was the real beginning of Women Together.

Beyond emergency aid, Women Together take Protestant and Catholic children on picnics together, open playgrounds and youth clubs, take meals to the elderly, and sponsor mixed groups on holidays. Love gives courage. A new dimension dawns in the life of a child who sees his mother stand shoulder-to-shoulder with the "enemy."

The hope is that Women Together can become the bridge over which both sides can learn to live together again in love and understanding — if not in this generation, in the generation of their children.

Why do people do such things? What activates that heavenly unrest within that triggers the need to alleviate the hurt, loneliness, sin, and suffering of another?

How do so many, so often, feel impelled to offer the gift of love appropriate to the need?

Is it perhaps because we were eyewitnesses of the most significant gift of love and serving that the world will ever know?

We were there in heaven when God the Father explained the plan of salvation and the creation of the world. He offered us, his children, the privilege of earth life, told us the role of Adam and Eve, and demonstrated the need for a Mediator to bring us back into his presence. We heard him ask, "Whom shall I send?" And we recognized the voice of our Elder Brother when he said: "Here I am, send me."

With those words Jesus Christ became the first volunteer. He volunteered to bless our lives eternally if we would choose to follow him and accept earth life with its opportunity to qualify for the highest degree of the celestial kingdom. He covenanted to do the will of the Father, to suffer in atoning for the sins of all mankind, to voluntarily give up his life upon the cross and take it up again after three days, that all his brothers and sisters might be redeemed from death.

We saw Satan step forward, saying, "Send me." But Satan's motives were not pure. The Savior's were; he chose to do the will of our Father, that the Father, not he, might be glorified.

And the Lord said, "I will send the first." (Abraham 3:27.)

"For God so loved the world, that he gave his only begotten Son, that whosoever believeth in him should not perish, but have everlasting life." (John 3:16.) We must have understood the importance and magnitude of love and desired to give a gift of love also. Was it then that we volunteered to share the burden of our Savior by asking the privilege to be our brother's keeper?

> Before the foundations of this earth were laid, a glorious decision was made allowing you and me to be our brother's keeper. By faith and service we would be able to achieve a degree of glory in the hereafter suited to our ... Christlike attainments. (Robert L. Simpson, *Conference Report*, April 1973.)

The vision of our responsibility to each other became dulled by our birth into earth life. But Father gives us opportunities to keep the covenant we made with one another. The Holy Ghost helps us to rediscover the way to love and serve as Father taught when we were nurtured near his side.

For me, one of those times of revelation came during a serious physical illness when, for a period of time, I lost my eyesight. As the pain in my eyes intensified, I became aware that the Spirit of the Lord was willing me to learn significant truths. I became acutely aware of my dependence on him. My need of my spirit brothers and sisters overwhelmed me; with tenderness and confidence born of training, they labored day and night to restore my health and strength that I might reclaim the joy and duties of a wife and mother. As my eyesight grew dimmer, my inner sight intensified. Love filled my soul and lifted it to a dimension of praise I had never before known.

One day I asked about my sight. I knew I would see again, for the servants of the Lord through the power of the Melchizedek Priesthood had given me his promise. But I needed to understand why I had become temporarily blind. The doctor answered my questions and talked about some of the physiological aspects of the eye. He explained that the eye has three scopes of vision: direct vision, peripheral vision, and panoramic vision.

"Direct vision," he said, "sees what is immediately in front of us. Peripheral vision is the ability to perceive images laterally that are not in our direct line of sight. Panoramic vision makes it possible for us to see a series of pictures representing a continuous scene as far as eye can see."

Lying there in total darkness I came to realize, through the inner light of the Spirit, that the vision of our responsibility to each other could be related to these three scopes of our eyesight.

Our direct vision of responsibility to each other reveals members of our immediate family. They are our personal responsibility. They hold first claim to our love, sacrifice, and service. Through prayer we are entitled to discover gifts of love we can give each other that no one outside the family circle can be sensitive to in just the same way. I believe one of the reasons why people are born into the same family is that each has been given gifts to fill the specific needs of another family member. Family ties give us the responsibility to respond to each other's needs.

Our peripheral vision of responsibility perceives friends and neighbors whose needs are revealed through the light of the Spirit. Our sincere concern for them can be evidenced by our living the baptismal covenant spoken of by Alma:

> And now, as ye are desirous to come into the fold of God, and to be called his people, and are willing to bear one another's burdens, that they may be light;
>
> Yea, and are willing to mourn with those that mourn; yea, and comfort those that stand in need of comfort, and to stand as witnesses of God at all times and in all things, and in all places that ye may be in, even until death, that ye may be redeemed of God, and be numbered with those of the first resurrection, that ye may have eternal life — (Mosiah 18:8-9.)

The sweeping panoramic vision of our responsibility to each other reveals all our spirit brothers and sisters who have ever lived, all who now walk the earth, and those who are yet to call this world home. Their spirits call to ours, and there stirs within us a desire to implement that glorious decision that made us our brother's keeper. Genealogical research and temple work are gifts we can give those who came to earth before we did and did not have the blessings of the gospel. We can live the gospel of Jesus, which is the gospel of love, and take that gospel to the whole world. To future generations we can give an honorable birth and a world made more Christlike by our gifts of love and service. "If there be eyes to see," said Elder S. Dilworth Young, "there will be visions to inspire."

Our motivation to alleviate one another's sorrow and suffering and share one another's joy is intrinsic, inherent within us, a like-child, like-Father attribute. That's why the people in the stories in this book, whose stories are grouped under the three visions of our responsibility to each other, found the need and gave their gift. The gift is love.

Our Personal Vision

The most important of the Lord's work you will ever do will be within the walls of your own home.

— Harold B. Lee

Greater Love Hath No Man

2

Most parents feel that if the necessity ever arose they would give their lives to save the lives of their children. Few are faced with that decision. Ryan's father was.

The rubber raft was sailing down the glassy river as smoothly as a huge duck. The sky was overcast. A cool, brisk wind was blowing from the northeast. Nine-year-old Ryan sighed contentedly as he turned over on his stomach to ease his sunburned back. He'd never been so utterly, ecstatically happy. He thought of his dad who had consented to let him run the river with him and with Travis, his older brother. "Dad's my very best friend," he thought. Then, he dozed.

The next thing he knew he was struggling for breath. Water was forming a whirlpool around him. He could hear someone screaming his name, but the current kept sucking his body down and down. There was a gurgling in his lungs; he thought his lungs would burst. He kept losing consciousness. Every time he came to the edge of giving up, someone called his name, and he would madly struggle upward.

Sixteen-year-old Travis made it to the river bank and pulled himself up over the sharp rocks. His right leg was bleeding, and he was sure his shoulder was broken. His eyes scanned the boiling river for his dad and for his little brother. He couldn't see either one of them.

It was all so sudden. Travis didn't know what had caused the raft to overturn. He was choking on regurgitated filth. He saw two men diving into the water. Then he saw Ryan, head and shoulders above the water. He looked as if he was just standing there. Travis struggled to scream his brother's name; no sound came. Just as he saw a man reach out to rescue Ryan, he fainted.

Travis and Ryan were taken to a small hospital and placed in beds, side by side. Ryan, who was in shock, had not wept nor uttered a word. Travis felt as though his heart would break. He tried but he could not penetrate Ryan's consciousness.

After an hour's silence, he said: "Ryan, did you see Dad after the boat overturned?"

Ryan began sobbing — great wracking sobs.

"Ryan, Ryan," Travis cried.

Finally Ryan quieted. "Travis," he said, "I was standing on Dad's shoulders."

After the water receded, the body of Ryan and Travis's father was found, his right foot wedged between two boulders.

3   A Gift That Blessed Mankind Eternally

The results of sharing spiritual experiences and bearing our testimonies to family members can echo throughout eternity. Andrew's gift of love to his brother is a dramatic example.

Andrew was a disciple of John the Baptist. One day as he and a friend were being taught by John, they looked up and saw Jesus approaching; and John said, "Behold the Lamb of God." Andrew was filled with the spirit of testimony, and he and his companion followed after Jesus. When Jesus became aware of them, he asked, "What seek ye?"

Desiring to continue following him, and fearing that they might lose sight of him, they asked the Savior where he lived. Jesus answered, "Come and see."

Having accepted the gracious invitation, Andrew went to find his brother so that he might share the joy of his discovery. "Come," Andrew said to Peter, "we have found the Messias."

Andrew took his brother to Jesus, and Jesus beheld him and said: "Thou art Simon, the son of Jona, thou shalt be called Cephas, which is, by interpretation, a seer, or a stone. (John 1:42, Inspired Version.)

Peter was destined to become President of the church of Jesus Christ, and as such he exercised all the keys of the kingdom of God for the blessing of the people in his generation and ours.

Andrew's sharing has had a powerful impact upon the functioning of the kingdom of God on the earth, and it will echo throughout eternity.

4 We Love Those Whom We Serve

When we become aware of the suffering of others and desire to help them change the direction of their lives, we need not feel inadequate because we are not learned in the methods and techniques of men. We but need to search the scriptures, diligently and thoughtfully, and our vision will be expanded and the way lighted before us. Jesus said: "Behold I am the light which ye shall hold up — that which ye have seen me do." (3 Nephi 18:24.)

The story of Jesus and the woman at the well is a good example of this truth.

The experience of Greg shows that when we have a sincere desire to help another we often follow the example of the Savior without being aware that that is what we are doing. What we do know, however, is that we feel good inside.

John relates the deeply moving experience of Jesus and the woman at the well, a touching teaching portrayal of giving and receiving. (John 4:5-42.) Each had something to give; each had a need to receive.

We can discover in these few short verses many truths that can lead us to be perceptive givers and receivers.

Jesus was traveling from Judea to Galilee. He was not compelled to go through Samaria. The Samaritans and the Jews were enemies. The disciples of Jesus must have been uneasy, wondering why he chose to go to the city of the enemy. But Jesus was following his own precept:

> But I say unto you, Love your enemies, bless them that curse you, do good to them that hate you, and pray for them which despitefully use you, and persecute you. (Matthew 5:44.)

In John's account the Savior exemplifies the courage to follow the promptings of the Spirit in showing love for our enemies even though it may mean venturing into enemy territory to reach those in need.

When Jesus reached the outskirts of Samaria, he was hungry, weary, and thirsty from the long day's journey. He sent his disciples to obtain food while he went alone to the well called Jacob's well. He "sat thus on the well," waiting for the one through whom he would reach many. Then "there cometh a woman of Samaria to draw water: Jesus saith unto her, Give me to drink."

Jesus, the Son of God, could have used his priesthood power to assuage his thirst, but he had committed to take upon himself all suffering, even the nettling needs of earth flesh.

His words "Give me to drink" can serve to help us realize that the erring one we are trying to reach will often more readily accept our sincere attempts to help him if we first elevate his self-esteem by asking him to serve us.

After accepting her gift of water, Jesus drew from the woman her need. With complete honesty he helped her face and admit her own dilemma. Though she did not immediately understand the depth and implication of his words, he guided her to verbalize her desire for water which would forever satisfy her thirst.

We hear her bearing testimony of the Messiah: "I know that the Messias cometh, which is called Christ: when he is come, he will tell us all things."

Her words emphasize the truth that even those who have made wrong choices, as she had done, often hold fast to some small seed of faith. Our gift can be to help them recognize that kernel of faith and encourage them to help it grow as Alma teaches. (See Alma 32:27.)

Jesus bore witness to the woman at the well that he was the Messiah. The woman then left her waterpot and went into the city and said to the men, "Come, see a man, which told me all things that ever I did: is not this the Christ?" And when others had come and seen and heard Jesus, they said to the woman: "Now we believe, not because of thy saying: for we have heard him ourselves, and know that this is indeed the Christ, the Saviour of the world."

A whole city was converted because Jesus made himself available to the one. He offered peace to the woman's troubled soul, but first he prepared the soil of her soul to hear.

Greg followed the example of the Savior's receiving and giving. Greg had not necessarily learned the truth illustrated in the story of Jesus and the woman at the well, but he was open to direction from the Holy Spirit.

The Garrards had accepted the challenge to be the foster family of a nineteen-year-old boy who was released from prison to a halfway house. There were nine Garrards, the parents and seven children. Every Thursday they piled into the station wagon for the forty-five-minute drive to the halfway house.

The second Thursday in May was one neither Greg nor Tommy will ever forget. Tommy had been acting like a brat for a week. Tessie, with the sophistication of a sixteen-year-old, commented: "Tommy certainly has a severe case of nine-year-old obnoxiousness, Mother. Can't you do something about him?"

Mother was well aware that something had to be done about Tommy. He had been unkind to the younger children and was sullen when she tried to talk to him. He stood with his chin sunk into his chest when his dad demanded that he "shape up."

By the time the family was settled in the station wagon, Dad was ready to spank Tommy. Mother had had it; her face was flushed with the effort of keeping her composure so that the evening would not be a total disaster.

Greg, Tommy's seventeen-year-old brother, sat next to him in the back seat. He was about to ram his elbow into Tommy's rib cage to motivate him to calm down when he saw that tears were running down the freckled face. Tommy looked straight ahead. An apple he had snitched on the way to the car bulged in his pocket. Greg knew Tommy would "catch it" if their parents saw that apple. The rule was "No food in the car."

Greg kept trying to get Tommy to talk, but he looked straight ahead and refused to speak. After several attempts to reach him, Greg thought, "Well, at least if Tommy would give me that apple he might be spared the spanking he's been asking for."

"Hey, give me that apple," Greg asked. Tommy got the message and dug out the apple. "Now," said Greg, "tell me what's the matter."

"Ah, you wouldn't care," Tommy replied, as he brushed the tears away with the back of his hand. "Nobody in this family cares about me. Nobody ever listens to me."

Greg felt shock. The realization hit him that the young former prisoner they were going to see had said approximately the same thing: "Nobody in my family ever really cared about me. Nobody ever listened."

Greg turned to Tommy: "Hey, I care. Come on, let's talk about it."

"You'd never understand," was Tommy's reply.

"Yes, I would. I promise I would, Tommy. Why, you're my brother. Try me and see." Greg felt sick. He had to get through. "Talk!" he demanded.

"Aw, you'd just laugh and bawl me out and tell all the others and they'd laugh, too."

Greg handed Tommy a crumpled tissue. Tommy made no effort to wipe away the tears. After a minute Greg reached over, took the tissue out of Tommy's hands, and wiped his face. "Look, Tommy," he said earnestly, "I promise I won't laugh or bawl you out or tell anyone. I love you, little buddy." Greg was serious. It was immensely important to him that he get through to Tommy and do whatever he could to help. He put his arm across the seat behind Tommy. He wanted to hug him, to pull him close, but he was afraid that would startle Tommy into crying out loud.

"Gee," thought Greg. "I can't remember hugging Tommy since he was about three." Now Greg himself felt like weeping. "I'm so busy doing my own thing that I don't even speak to some of the little kids for days at a time — unless they get in the way or something; and then I'm rough and growl at them." Greg didn't feel good about that discovery. He fidgeted in his seat.

Then Greg deliberately let his arm slip down around Tommy's shoulder. For a minute Tommy sat rigid, his hands clenched in his lap. Then he said disconsolately: "Well, you always got *A*'s in math. You'd think a kid was just plain stupid if he was failing math."

"Ouch!" thought Greg, "that hurt! It hurt because it's true; sure enough I'd laugh and call him a dumb-dumb. Boy, I could be responsible for making Tommy feel just like that fellow we're going to see!" After a silence, he asked quietly, "Tommy, are you failing math?"

"What do you care?" Tommy replied, but he relaxed a little.

"I do care. I care a lot." ("I'll have to do more than say so," Greg thought.) "Tell you what, Tommy, I'll help you till you catch on. Math's not hard once you get the hang of it — it can be downright exciting!" ("I didn't know I liked math that much," Greg said to himself.)

"You would?" Tommy's voice was incredulous.

"You can depend on it," Greg was sincere.

This happened three years ago. Tommy is not a whiz at math, but he's average. The great thing about him is that he's almost always kind and thoughtful toward his younger brothers and sisters. He remembers that Greg pointed out that unacceptable actions can be symptoms of a need rather than of meanness.

Greg is now on a mission. Of all his brothers and sisters, he misses Tommy the most. We love the most those whom we serve the most.

Greg was reminiscing on that situation with Tommy when his missionary companion interrupted his thoughts with "Hurry up! Let's go to Mrs. Trythall's and approach her for the sixth time to listen to the gospel lessons."

A thought popped into Greg's mind. Surreptitiously he tugged at a loose button on his topcoat. It came off in his hand. "Okay," he said, "but first I'm going to ask her to sew a button on my coat. To give a little gift of love might open her heart."

5 Love Suffereth Long

It took years for Maribeth and Bill to learn to live in love. When they did, they found healing; and on its wings they found an immediate need to exercise that "love that never faileth" for the strengthening of one of their children.

"I believe," said Elder Marvin J. Ashton, "we start to fail in the home when we give up on each other. We have not failed until we have quit trying. As long as we are working diligently with love, patience, and long-suffering, despite the odds or the apparent lack of progress, we are not classified as failures in the home. We only start to fail when we give up on a son, daughter, mother, or father." (Ensign, June 1971, pages 31-32.)

For thirteen years Maribeth suffered because of her husband's alcohol problem. At first she tried to ignore Bill's drinking; he desperately seemed to need to keep his problem from her. She was terrified and felt helpless to cope.

Though she tried to keep their home functioning, her surface composure was merely a facade. Underneath, she was alternately bewildered, ashamed, angry, and despondent. The effort took its toll. She looked tired and careworn most of the time. She thought she was protecting their two children from the knowledge of their father's drinking. When he came home glassy-eyed, uncertain of gait, she told them he was sick or working too hard and must be left alone. It wasn't easy for the children; they loved their father and needed him, but they stayed away from him. They never asked questions, but the questions were always there — in their eyes.

Ten-year-old John thought that somehow he was to blame for the dark secret of his father's actions. Increasing behavioral problems were symptomatic of his confusion. When a situation arose that eight-year-old Mari couldn't handle, she took refuge in becoming sick.

One late afternoon Maribeth stood in the doorway absentmindedly watching the children playing in the backyard. Suddenly her plastic world was shattered. Timmy, the ten-year-old neighbor boy, began staggering around, talking in a loud voice, slurring his words together. "Look! 'shee' me, I'm playing I'm your dad." He continued his exaggerated antics, unaware that John and Mari stood dead still, their faces frozen in horror.

John came to life first. His face distorted with rage, he ran to Timmy and began blindly striking out at him with his fist. He screamed, "My dad's sick! Sick!" Mari came running to her mother. "My stomach," she wailed. Maribeth rushed her to the bathroom. Then she ran out and disengaged John from a thoroughly frightened Timmy. She sent Timmy home and took John in the house, wiped his tears and washed his face.

The children were silent as Maribeth prepared their dinner and helped them into their pajamas. She felt as though her tongue was glued to the roof of her mouth. What little respect she had had for Bill was extinguished. Trying to keep their trouble from the world was no longer important. She was filled with dread and hatefulness. To hurt her was one thing, but to cause the children suffering was another. She felt she could never forgive him.

After the children were in bed, she began to map out a plan. Ten years later Maribeth was to admit that when she finally went into action she did all the wrong things.

When Bill came home, she was too wrapped up in her own misery to notice that he was sober. He had lost his fourth job in three years. The minute he walked in she began telling him, through clenched teeth, that he was a disgrace to her and to the children, that he was no good to her or to them, and that she wanted him to pack his things and get out. Bill stalked out of the house, only to return the next day drunk and abusive. He refused to move out of their home.

From that time on Maribeth no longer tried to shield their plight from the world. She needed support and direction. She got sympathy and attention. Most people aligned themselves with her. Their friends told her how wonderful she was to put up with Bill. Some, behind her back, said she was a fool to stay with him, and others said that she probably was the cause of Bill's drinking. Maribeth never tired of telling people how often she and the children prayed for Bill. She developed a "holier than thou" attitude and, without realizing it, played the role of a self-righteous martyr. This increased Bill's sense of guilt, and he drank himself into oblivion more frequently than ever.

The children didn't have the defense mechanism Maribeth had. John grew sullen and rebellious. He alternated between hate for his mother and hate for his father. He became a loner and refused to go to Church activities. He couldn't handle the sympathy and the "you poor, dear boy" attitude of some who meant well. He heard the mother of one of his few friends say to her son, "You don't want to associate with him, his dad's an alcoholic." John assumed that every parent in the area thought the same. Periodically he ran away from home, each time to be brought back by the police. Mari fared a little better, but she was fast becoming a neurotic. Whenever a situation she couldn't handle arose at home or at school, she automatically became sick.

Maribeth's "wonderful woman" image helped her in some ways. She was sincere in her desire to be what people said she was. She began studying the gospel, and she tried to teach it to her children. She tried to have family prayer and family home evening but gave up when the children didn't cooperate. She became involved in Church activities. Though she did not see herself honestly, in her way she was sincerely trying to be a better person.

Bill's continued drinking caused him to suffer all the classic symptoms of the alcoholic. He began hallucinating, he experienced memory loss, and he developed alcoholic pellagra. One day he collapsed on the street and was taken to a hospital. His life was in danger. Slowly, as his system became free of alcohol, he admitted to the hospital social worker that he wanted to be sober more than he wanted to be drunk.

Two days later when Bill awoke from a long sleep, a man and his wife were sitting by his bed. They introduced themselves as Jerry and Lorene Jackson. They told him they were volunteers. Bill said, "Hello," then drifted off to sleep again, wondering what a couple of squares like the Jacksons thought they could do for him. When he awoke an hour later, Jerry Jackson was still sitting there.

Bill didn't feel much like being civil. He blurted out: "Look, it's nice of you to come, but I don't think you're going to like me. You look as if you've lived your life in a little ivory tower. I don't need any do-gooders. You wouldn't know about people like me. If I don't make it this time, I'm going to blow my head off, so just go away."

Jerry Jackson stood up, walked over to the bed, put his hand on Bill's shoulder, and looked straight into his eyes. "Bill," he said gravely, "you'd better have meant it when you said you were ready for help. I'm here to help, but I want you to know one thing — don't ever try to con me, because I know my way around your head. I've been there."

That was the beginning of Bill's slow, painful reentry into the life of the living. It was a seesaw battle. Jerry Jackson had an uncanny way of knowing when Bill needed help. He showed up at odd times, sometimes staying for a few minutes, other times for an hour or two. One Saturday night three months after Bill had been released from the hospital, Jerry knocked on the door at 10:30 P.M. He stayed all night, all the next day, and into the evening. At one point Jerry thought he'd have to "slug" Bill to keep him from breaking out of the house to find a drink. Bill cursed and insulted him. Jerry paid no attention. Finally, Jerry got Bill on his knees for the fourth time, but this time Bill took his turn in verbal prayer. When it was over, Bill cried for twenty minutes. Bill and Jerry both knew the battle would never be quite so hard or quite so terrible again.

As Bill struggled to become well, Maribeth found she was having a more difficult time than she'd had in all the years Bill had been drinking. She was hateful, spiteful, and at times downright mean. She felt animosity toward Jerry because he was successful in helping Bill when she had never seemed to reach him with all her self-sacrificing prayers, preachings, and threats and accusations of "If you loved me and the children, you'd quit."

Lorene, Jerry's wife, tried to befriend her, to give her reassurance and advice; but Maribeth was so antagonistic that she was difficult to reach.

One day Lorene dropped in unexpectedly. Maribeth was angry. She blurted out all her hard feelings and frustrations. She told Lorene that she didn't appreciate Jerry coming to their home so often; he was taking Bill's time, and Bill was becoming dependent on him. When Maribeth paused for breath, Lorene quietly said, "If Bill had a dread disease, would you be jealous of the doctor who was trying to make him well?"

Maribeth was shocked. For the first time she recognized that she needed help as much as Bill did. Sitting across from her was a woman who not only could give help, but was offering it. Later Maribeth expressed the situation in this way:

"When I saw myself honestly, I was aghast. Lorene taught me the meaning of Paul's words:

> Charity suffereth long, and is kind; charity envieth not; charity vaunteth not itself, is not puffed up, doth not behave itself unseemly, seeketh not her own, is not easily provoked, thinketh no evil; rejoiceth not in iniquity, but rejoiceth in the truth; beareth all things, believeth all things, hopeth all things, endureth all things. (1 Corinthians 13:4-7.)

She pleaded with me to put this into practice. I've tried. The results have been unbelievable.

"After several weeks of struggle, fasting and praying, calling Lorene when I needed direction and encouragement, and talking to the bishop, I began to see myself as I was. Last Tuesday I went to Bill and with love asked for his forgiveness and his help. As I did so, I was prompted to ask him to give me a husband's blessing. We put our arms around each other, and for the first time in years we felt like husband and wife. We both cried. He asked me to fast and pray with him in preparation for giving me a blessing.

"The following week, in the privacy of our bedroom, he gave me the first husband's blessing I have ever had. I cannot share in words what it meant to us both. I do know it has become a ballast in our lives, a memory, a cleansing, a strength we can remember when the going gets tough. I wish I could say I have changed overnight. I haven't, but love is becoming part of me and my peace is growing."

Bill gradually began to take over his responsibility as head of the home. With the help of a friend of Jerry's, he found a job. It was hard, outdoor labor. Bill recognized it was the kind of physical exertion he needed. Jerry challenged him to read a chapter from the New Testament each day. Some days he read two. He lived an hour at a time and kept praying.

One Sunday, Bill ventured to priesthood meeting. He purposely went late. Some of the men saw him and looked quickly away. When the bishop noticed him, he smiled and nodded. Bill didn't stay for class, but later that day the elders quorum president came to see him and offered to pick him up the next Sunday morning. Bill told him he would let him know. Four weeks later he walked into priesthood meeting on his own and stayed through the meeting. The men in his quorum had been conditioned. They welcomed him sincerely. Gradually Bill became active in his ward. He looked like a different man, happy and more self-confident. Two years later he became ward financial clerk.

Maribeth and Bill are now a husband-and-wife team in their home, church, and community. They spend hours helping others who have problems. They are more effective than most because of what they have learned through their own suffering. They see Jerry and Lorene often. Theirs is an eternal friendship.

What about Maribeth and Bill's children? Mari will be all right. Maribeth and Bill have worked with her and pointed out to her that she becomes sick when she can't handle her emotions. They reinforce her through good-natured humor. Her efforts to see her actions honestly and to control them before they control her are paying off. She has made great strides; she can even laugh at herself at times.

John — dear, sensitive John — needs all the help and understanding his parents can give. He often comes home drunk.

Maribeth and Bill learned from Lorene and Jerry the strength of love coupled with determined perseverance. Bill says, "God never gave up on me — we'll never give up on John."

6 When a Little Child Comes Bearing Gifts

The Savior in his statement "a little child shall lead them" reminds us that little children have much to give and that their gifts should be valued. Their spontaneity in giving and loving is Christlike. It would be a more beautiful world, a more peaceable kingdom, if we could resist the pressure of sophistication and preserve the joy of childlike giving.

David was destined to be a "little child" all his mortal life. His talent was discovered and developed, his gift given, because so many people unselfishly gave to him.

Sherrie, Bonnie, and David were born into the same family. They were beautiful children. Theirs was a warm, close-knit family, responsive to each other's needs.

When David was barely three years old, tests showed that he was mentally retarded. Sherrie and Bonnie wept and vowed they would never be ashamed of their beautiful little brother. David's mother assessed the situation honestly. Her understanding deepened for those who are ill, misunderstood, or different. She became diligent in her efforts to soften the shock and alleviate the deep hurt of other mothers in like circumstances. David's father, a quiet, soft-spoken man, determined that their son should be given every opportunity to learn and fulfill his potential, limited as it would be in earth life.

David was a happy, sunshiny little boy. As he approached teen years, he somehow knew he was not the same as other children. He was often sad and frustrated because of his inability to concentrate for very long or to coordinate his mind and body. He was, however, a plucky youngster and learned to dress himself. He did routine chores around the home — emptied the wastebaskets, raked the lawn, vacuumed the carpet, and washed the windows. He took pride in remembering to do his daily duties and was especially pleased when complimented.

His parents wisely enrolled him in a school for special children. When he was twenty-two he learned a trade. He became a carpenter's helper. Though his tasks were few and routine, he was a dependable, good-natured employee.

His response to the smooth, beautiful wood was extraordinary for a person as limited as David. He often lovingly caressed a smooth piece of wood with the flat of his hand. He would sniff its rich, spicy odor. He noted patterns and imagery; unusual wood grains intrigued him. Mr. Johnson, one of the older carpenters, noticed David's appreciation and was impressed with the imaginative way he spoke about the unusual designs exposed when a piece of wood was cut.

It was Mr. Johnson who first introduced David to the delight of wood carving. During their lunch hour, Mr. Johnson's gray head and David's blond, tousled one could be seen bent over some carving on which Mr. Johnson was working. David's face was rapt with delight as he watched. One day Mr. Johnson gave David a box of soft balsam wood and an old wood-carving knife. As David fingered the wood and rubbed it with his hand, into his eyes came a faraway look — he was dreaming of the shapes the wood could take if he could carve. It was weeks before he mustered the courage to try. Wisely, Mr. Johnson did not urge him. He let David watch him, answered his questions, and put the pieces into his hands so that he could examine the carvings and trace them with his sensitive fingers.

Then one day David began. He took the carving knife and

with an audible sigh made a few cuts and scratches on the wood. Each day, half fearful, half delighted, he would try to fashion the wood into the shape of the dream in his head. After many months of patient and repeated attempts, he handed Mr. Johnson a clumsily wrapped package. It was David's first finished wood carving — the figure of a small dog, ears back, running into the wind. It was a crude effort, but there was a certain fluid beauty in the body and head of the little dog.

Mr. Johnson could hardly believe his eyes. He recognized that David had talent. With his old felt hat in his hands, sawdust on his shoes and in his moustache, and his eyes shining with earnestness, he called on David's parents. He told them of David's dependability and tenacity in his work. He spoke tenderly of David's love for wood. Then he took from his pocket the little carving. David's parents took turns holding the treasure. His father touched it gently; his mother surreptitiously wiped a tear from her cheek. Then they turned and looked into the face of their puzzled son. When he saw that the little dog pleased them, he beamed proudly and stood taller.

With great effort, David began to carve small, primitive figures, not realizing the beauty and motion in his carvings. Some of his figures were displayed and readily sold by one of the town's nicer gift shops. Not all of David's carvings were for sale. He proudly presented some of them to people who, at various times, had been kind to him. Those who received the gifts marveled over them and cherished them. Among the recipients was a man just older than David who had often pulled David in his little red wagon when they were little boys. David never seemed to forget those who cared about him, felt comfortable with him, and accepted him as a person worthy of notice.

David's parents came to realize that he needed associations beyond what they could give. They recognized his need to relate to others on his own level. For the last five years of his life, David lived in a home with other retarded people. They contributed to their own livelihood and to each other's happiness. David's eyes lost their hurt, bewildered look. He had accepted the talents given him and magnified them. He contributed beauty to a world in need of beauty.

When we come to make an accounting of our talents, no doubt we will be reminded that "where much is given, much is expected." David's contribution cannot be measured against someone else's; it is his, unique to him. His world and his contribution to it may have been restricted through no fault of his, but he magnified the talents that were given him.

David died when he was thirty-two years old. He is buried in a grassy spot, secluded from the street. Marking his grave is a lovely wooden marker, beautifully carved by old Mr. Johnson. It reads: "David, My Friend." At the top of the marker is the figure of a little dog, ears back, running into the wind.

Children have a natural tendency to fulfill certain commandments without realizing that they are doing so. Perhaps they have not lived with the world so long that the teachings "of [their] former friends and birth" have become dulled and forgotten.

Anne did not realize she was keeping the specific commandment: "Pure religion and undefiled before God and the Father is this, To visit the fatherless and widows in their affliction. . . ." (James 1:27.)

Anne's twelfth birthday was, in her words, "The most special, beautiful birthday of my whole entire life." She had asked her parents if she could have two birthday gifts: (1) her patriarchal blessing; and (2) that as a family they take a program to the nursing home in their small town. Her father and mother were deeply touched. Together the family decided on a program agenda. Peter, ten years old, would play the piano. Anne would play her violin. Steven, five, and Danny, four, would sing. Mother would accompany them on the piano. Father, a busy doctor, would act as master of ceremonies.

On the day of Anne's birthday, just before they left for the nursing home, Mother and Anne cut eighteen roses from the rose garden and wrapped their stems in wet paper towels. There was a beautiful rose for each of the widows in the nursing home.

The program was well received. After the family had given their gifts, Anne asked the women if they would like to join them in singing a song. They requested "Love at Home." Danny directed; using both hands, he added flourishes Eugene Ormandy would have envied.

There were both laughter and tears as the happy family said goodbye.

"Let's do it again on my birthday," cried a happy Peter.

"Ours too," the little boys echoed.

Mother squeezed Anne's hand.

It was a day of giving, fasting, and rejoicing for Anne and her family. In the evening, at the appointed hour, she received her patriarchal blessing.

I've often wondered if Brian's gift — his reason for being born — was to open the door of heaven and leave it ajar so that his parents could see in.

Anita saw the doctor coming up the long corridor. His shoulders were stooped, his head bent forward. In her heart she knew the news was not good. She reached out to her husband and he put his arm around her. The contact steadied her. The doctor's face was tired and drawn. "Your son has leukemia."

Anita and Paul didn't realize it then, but as one door was closed to them another was opened.

They took Brian home to die. In the days that followed, Anita felt sorrow like heavy ingots of iron pulling her soul down into an abyss of despair. The bishop came, and the Relief Society president organized the sisters to bring in food. Anita was grateful. She and Paul had never been particularly active in the Church. They weren't against the Church; they just didn't really care.

After the home teachers came and administered to Brian they would go out to weed the flower beds and cut the lawn. Paul was grateful and relieved. He spent most of his time with their two daughters, Diane and Marcy. They were bewildered and bitter. Brian was their only brother.

"Brian," Anita realized, "is the only one who has peace." The thought made her cry.

Anita was not sure when Brian began talking about the Savior. To each family member he spoke privately and quietly. At first Anita wasn't hearing what he said. She did not want to accept the truth that he was drawing near the other side. After a day or two she realized that his words were simple, his meaning profound. He was telling them that the Savior loved them and him. He was accepting his suffering with a degree of fortitude surprising in one ten years old.

Paul was most affected. He implored them all to listen to Brian and consider what he was saying.

One evening, about sundown, Brian seemed restless. When Anita asked if she could do something for him to make him more comfortable, he said, "Call Daddy." Anita almost cried out, but Brian's imploring look made her realize she must be strong for his sake.

Paul stood by one side of the bed, Anita by the other. At Brian's request they each took one of his hands. For a while Brian closed his eyes as if he were sleeping, while Paul and Anita watched him, weeping quietly. Finally he opened his eyes. "Daddy, Mother," he said softly, "please go to the temple and be married. If you do, we will be a family for always."

"We will," said Paul, his voice tearful and sincere. He meant it.

"You will, won't you, Mother?" Brian said, pleadingly.

"Of course we will," Anita answered, and laid her lips on

his little hot forehead. "We will," she said to herself, and her heart softened. Though one door was closing, the door to the celestial kingdom was slightly ajar.

Brian looked up into their faces and smiled. His whole face seemed illumined with an inner light.

He slept for a while, then opened his eyes. "I love you," he said, and drifted off to sleep.

At 4:15 A.M. the next morning he opened his eyes, smiled a beautiful, angelic smile, and slipped away.

7 Sanctification Is a Process

Everyone has a gift to give, even those who are invalids. No one but Heavenly Father knows how deeply invalids suffer by being the object of so much necessary service, but they too serve. Sanctification is a process, and Father knows which process, serving or being served, can give each of us the opportunity to come back into his presence.

Christy's mother and Carmen bless the lives of those who care for them; not in the way they would choose to bless the lives of those they love, but in the way Father requires.

I have a precious friend, Carmen, who is afflicted with multiple sclerosis. She once said to me: "I used to be vain about my appearance. Worldly possessions and pride of social position were extremely important to me. Not any more. I'm learning some difficult lessons. I've had to accept being an object of pity because of the condition of my body. I have come to accept acts of charity with graciousness. My children, some not yet in their teens, must wait on me and care for me physically, as I did for them when they were babies. I wish it didn't have to be this way. I ache to serve them as most mothers are privileged to do.

"The hardships and heartaches have made me a better person. I try daily to learn what the Lord would have me learn. You see, I'd rather become worthy to walk in his presence than be beautiful, socially prominent, or famous. I have often wondered if I would have reached the depth of commitment in any other way. Does it really matter what we suffer if we qualify to live with him? Pray for me; don't pray for my suffering to be less, but that I may endure to the end regardless of what is required."

Once a week for ten years Shirley and Jean have given practical gifts of service to Carmen and her family. Once a week Shirley cleans Carmen's home, scrubs floors and bathroom fixtures, washes woodwork and windows, and does whatever else is needed. Jean does the weekly shopping for groceries and personal items for Carmen. Shirley and Jean are two beautiful women, affluent, and busy in the Church and community. They don't talk about what they do for Carmen. Few people know. They're not on an ego trip. Carmen needs them. They care about her. Their gift may not always be convenient to give, week after week, but it is given. Shirley and Jean know they receive far beyond the cost of the gifts.

Over the years, many people have served Carmen. She often says: "One of my prayers is that my contribution to the eternal lives of those who serve me, family, friends, and ward members, will be that the services they give me, in love, with faithful repetition, sometimes with impatience, will prove to be a part of their eternal growth."

Christy's mother is the victim of a massive stroke. Christy writes:

"Mother is completely paralyzed. The only part of her anatomy she can move are her eyes and eyelids. Her mind is sharp. She can hear, and she communicates by blinking 'yes' or 'no.'

"Before her illness Mother was a good listener. We joke with her now about there not being a better listener than she because she can't interrupt.

"After over nine years of complete paralysis, Mother still communicates her deep love and concern for her family and friends.

"I often ask myself: 'Why is my mother paralyzed? Why Mother?' She has a son and a daughter and eight grandchildren. She's the wife of a stake president. Her life has been dedicated to serving, graciously and gladly — sensitive to individual tastes and needs. She has a testimony of the gospel. She loves the Savior. She has lived a beautiful, useful life.

"I think what it would be like not to be able to say, 'Thank you,' 'I'm in pain,' 'I love you.' Not to be able to hug a grandchild you used to swing in your arms out in the backyard by your rose garden while singing, 'I love Wendy.'

"Because of what you are, your family can't clearly recall what you were. You are a totally different you.

"Strangers and old friends have no idea how to visit and talk with you because you can't respond in any way except to blink. It takes practice and a husband nearby to help others learn how to ask questions that can be answered correctly with a blink.

"For four and a half years after Mother became paralyzed, she and Dad lived in our home. Dad had to adjust to our young family. He was away from old friends and his own ward. Our ward consisted of very young families.

"We had to find nurses. It takes a long time to find the right kind. When we cannot endure another day without more sleep, the need is filled — almost always with the 'just right' person. Sometimes nurses become ill and can't come at the last minute, and there we are doing a night shift with no nap and a big meeting the next day.

"It takes weeks to train each new nurse. Mother must have a nurse twenty-four hours a day because she can't swallow all the time; she could choke to death if someone isn't there to use the suction machine to remove the mucus. There are so many little details that must be learned, and Mother can't help the nurse know what to do or how to do it, so it's double duty for someone until they learn.

"Bless the nurses! They become very committed to Mother — close, dear friends. They have to become emotionally involved. Sometimes they can nearly read Mother's mind. Each is very dear and special in her own way. They go many extra miles and hours. They say that they enjoy the peace and beautiful spirit in her room.

"Dad is always improving techniques, timing, and medication for Mother. He worked eight hours a day, plus overtime at payroll and tax time. He shops for special nursing items for Mom. Dad has stayed up all night on many occasions to keep Mom comfortable.

"Our children learned early the meaning of sacrifice. They would say: 'Mom, if you don't have to tend Grannie ...'; or, 'If you will be free, could we do this?'; or, 'Could you come to this school function?' Naturally they had dozens of requests, but Grannie came first.

"Each of the children learned how to 'tend' Grannie. Mike, sixteen, would get up early in the morning and take the shift that was the hardest because most of the family never got to sleep before midnight. Kenny, twenty, ran errands and helped in numerous ways. Wendy, fourteen, played the piano for Grannie and learned to help with the cooking while still small. Lowell, eleven, saved his money to buy thoughtful gifts and was generally helpful and always cheerful. Sandra, nine, loved everybody; she now makes special disposable bibs for Grannie.

"Tamara, nineteen, now takes care of Mom on Saturday mornings; she has helped with Grannie's care since seventh-grade days. Grannie is very interested in what each child is doing, and Tamara tries to tell her things I might forget. Tamara takes her dates to visit Grannie so that Grannie can 'check them out.' She says that it's like walking into a chapel when she goes there. She often declares: 'A great part of my testimony has come through working with Grannie. Working with her and trying to be in tune with her spirit to discover her needs is like praying or being in tune with the Lord's Spirit.'

"My husband is devoted to Mother. He built a shower bath so that she could be showered. He is patient and helpful. My love for him has deepened. He has sacrificed privacy and the kind of home life husbands rightfully expect.

"It's very hard to live with the feeling that we've never done all we could for Mother. Is she really comfortable? We've all gone to bed thinking about her and being more aware of our own comfort. Is there a good book someone has partially read to her that she would like finished? Would she prefer TV, talk, or quiet? Has she developed a cramp, a headache, an itch since you last talked? Is she sick to death of the questions?

"Then, for me, there is the emotional strain of trying to be daughter, nurse, wife, mother, housekeeper, cook, wash-woman, Church worker — not in any special order but all at the same time. It has been difficult to help the many welcome visitors deal with their reactions and emotional stress.

"We have all grown and benefited from this experience. We have each discovered that we have our own special gift to give Mother. I don't have a talent for giving a soothing backrub, but I've studied nutrition and developed a formula that is fed to her through a tube. It has maintained Mother's weight and general health. The doctors marvel that she has never had a bedsore, thanks to meticulous nursing care, diet, and the vitamins Dad includes with her medication.

"Of course, Dad is the key to the whole operation. Without him, it couldn't be done. Five and a half years ago Dad rented an apartment in their old neighborhood, near old and dear friends. Several women volunteered to learn how to care for Mother, so Dad was assured that Mother was cared for when nurses or family could not be there. These good women have helped to lift the financial burden, especially since the insurance ran out. They are dependable and devoted. They consider it a privilege to serve another.

"Time passes, faith is exercised, many prayers are said and many administrations and blessings are given, but Mother's body is still the same — completely paralyzed. Her mind con-tinues to be clear. She can hear, think, blink her 'yeses' and 'noes.' For her, for us, for all who are enduring with her, the experience is painfully strengthening — like steel being tempered in the heat of a fiery furnace. I've wished I could quickly perfect myself so that the Lord would allow me to go through it for her, then I could quit trying to imagine what she endures.

"Mother's testimony has always been strong. She bore it in Church often and talked to us about it, but the time it meant the most to me was when one of her friends, who sings in the Mormon Tabernacle Choir, came to visit. She sang a number of songs for Mother. It came time for her to leave, but Mom would not give her a 'good-bye' blink. Dad kept asking questions until he finally determined that there was one more song she wanted to hear. One of us thought of the right answer — 'I Know That My Redeemer Lives.' Mom blinked 'yes,' and her friend sang it. Dad said, 'She wanted to bear her testimony and now it has been done for her.' Mother blinked in agreement. The words of Job, no doubt, help Mother to live on and endure to the end:

> For I know that my redeemer liveth, and that he shall stand at the latter day upon the earth:

> And though after my skin worms destroy this body, yet in my flesh shall I see God. (Job 19:25-26.)

"Recently, at the insistence of one of the volunteers, Dad fixed a bed in the volunteer's camper, eye-level to the windows so that Mother could see out. At first they took Mother for short drives around the city. Then they took a trip to Las Vegas to visit my brother, who was attending a convention there. The next spring they drove across the country to his home in Atlanta, Georgia, to see a new grandson. Two nurses accompanied them on each trip.

"As a family member said, 'If you love someone enough you can do anything,' and Dad has. But knowing Dad, he will still come up with something new — something to widen the horizons of Mother's prison.

"And loving them both as we do, we will all do what we can to help."

The Gifts of Eternal Giving

As we grow older, we can come to believe that we are useless. Many elderly in the world are robbed of their self-respect because some younger people have come to believe that the old are liabilities and have nothing to give. Yet we often observe older people who are busy, happy, even exuberant about the challenges the sunset years bring.

> Even the oldest tree some fruit
>   may bear; ...
> For age is opportunity no less
> Than youth itself ...
>
> — Henry Wadsworth Longfellow

I went to the temple at six o'clock one Wednesday morning. The chapel was crowded with elderly people. Their faces shone, their eyes sparkled. Their spirits were at peace. I spoke about it to one of the officiators. "Yes, they are beautiful," he said. "Most of them come every morning and stay all day doing work for their kindred dead. They are happy because they are offering the gift of eternal lives to those who have gone before. Usually, they do temple work for their own kindred whose genealogical work they've done."

A few days later I saw a televised news special about aging people in a distant state. Many older people who were sick, despondent, abandoned, and hopeless were simply waiting to die.

I found myself thinking of those contented, beautiful people I'd seen in the temple.

My husband asked why I was weeping. "For all the lost and lonely older people," I said, "who still have gifts to give and no one to give them to."

9 The Circle of Concern

Brampton was a "just me" person. He didn't want anyone, not even the Lord, to get near enough to become involved in his little world. He thought he was self-sufficient. He was non-praying and proud; nothing must stand in the way of his dream.

Brampton postponed giving love and concern until it was too late, as far as his children were concerned.

I once read a poster that was thumbtacked to the livingroom wall of a small apartment shared by four girls. I wish I knew the person who wrote it. It reminds me of all the Bramptons in the world.

"People so seldom say 'I love you,'
And when they do it's either too late or love has gone;
So when I say 'I love you,' it doesn't mean you'll never go,
It only means I wish you didn't have to."

Brampton wanted all his life to be a physician and surgeon. He came from a home where the necessities of life were hard-earned. He made up his mind while still a boy that someday he would be rich. After many severe struggles he became a competent doctor and set up his practice in an affluent neighborhood.

His dedication paid off in money but robbed him of life's most precious possession — his family. He had not time for his wife and three children. They, in turn, built their daily lives without thought of him, except for what he could give them materially. Money was the center of his universe — the circumference of the tight little circle that imprisoned him. He wrote checks to get the family "off his back." He was proud he had money. He flaunted it.

One winter day his two sons and his daughter died in an airplane crash while vacationing in Beirut. In his shock he repeated over and over again: "But I never knew them — I always intended to become acquainted with them. Now I will never know their dreams, nor understand what made them sad or happy. I shall never know if they loved me or even if they will miss me. I am not a success — I have failed."

His wife, in her suffering, cried out to him. "You are blind in your grief and I am deaf and dumb in mine. Please help me!"

But they had no foundations from which to reach each other. They became vindictive, spiteful, and hurtful to each other when each needed the other's support. They separated. Divorce was discussed.

A little girl who was dying of a rare bone disease helped Brampton to see that, though his children were gone, there were others who needed his love and personal concern.

He was called as a consultant to determine whether a bone transplant would prolong five-year-old Mary Alice's life. It was too late; surgically he could do nothing. But he did not turn away from her when he knew his skill was useless, as had been his pattern in the past. He visited the little girl often, bringing small gifts. He was with her when she died. Just before death came, she looked up at him and said, "I love you."

"I love you, too," he said.

Somehow in that moment Brampton came to realize that his wife loved him and needed him. He had not given her love or sympathy. He discovered he needed her. That was a new emotion for him. For a month he lived with his need. His soul became raw with suffering. Finally he went to her and expressed his need. They wept in each other's arms.

They are growing closer to each other because they are

helping each other grow. They have come to the realization that in their children's deaths are ties to heaven which are deep and real — almost tangible. A submission to and faith in the Lord Jesus Christ has come into their souls.

They are discovering new meaning in life. They have become caring people. Other caring people are drawn to them. They are in the process of creating a place for themselves by responding to the suffering of others.

Brampton's reputation is changing. Among his colleagues he is beginning to be known as one anxious and ready to offer his skills of healing, regardless of the monetary benefits. Brampton gives his gifts for love's sake.

10 The Flight of the Lamanite Boy

April Star knew sacrifice – aching, hurting sacrifice. She gave up her son to a world she could not know or understand, but through her suffering she gave the gift of a brighter forever to him and his children after him.

In the life of April Star and her son, Hawk in Flight, we see prophecy becoming reality.

"And thus we see that the Lord began to pour out his Spirit upon the Lamanites, because of their easiness and willingness to believe in his words." (Helaman 6:36.)

April Star had ridden for an hour over rutted, bumpy roads in the back of the old pickup truck. The child within her kicked in protest, but her mind was not with the soon-to-be-born child but with her eldest son, nine-year-old Hawk in Flight, who was coming home for the summer from the white man's school.

She wondered if he now preferred his white parents' home to the Indian hogan. She had missed him fiercely. Some mornings she had arisen before dawn and walked into the desert, seeking surcease from the longing for her firstborn. She remembered his birth, her pride in his sturdy body, and his beautiful eyes. She had often gone without food when he was little so he could fill his little brown belly. When he went away last fall, he was a head taller than most of the children born in the year of his birth. She thought of the times she had joined him on the hillside as he watched the few lean sheep. He was responsible and wise for one so young. When he spoke, she listened and wondered about the man inside him.

When he was still little, she had worried about him growing up and becoming like some of the young Indian men she had seen in town on Saturday nights — drunken, slovenly, loud-mouthed, swearing, and disrespectful. The stories of young men sent away to jail for stealing frightened her. How could she guard him from the liquor and the breaking of the white man's laws? How could she keep him apart from the girls and women whose purpose it was to get money and to lead young men into sin and disease?

In her heart she had said: "Hawk in Flight must learn to read and write. He must prepare to live in the white man's world. He must live in a house with glass windows and curtains. He must learn so that his children will not know hunger as we do." But there were no schools, and she could not teach him because she could not read or write. Before she knew how to pray to the Lord, she would look into the sun and chant long prayers for him.

A warm light shone in her eyes as she thought about the evening two years ago when two young men approached the hogan. Her heart had beat fast. She had heard about the "gamalii." They were missionaries of The Church of Jesus Christ of Latter-day Saints. After that first evening, they came often to tell her and her family the story of the red men of the Book of Mormon. She, her husband, and the grandmother had listened, but it was eight-year-old Hawk in Flight who under-stood and explained. Curiosity turned to belief. They were baptized and confirmed.

One day she learned about the LDS Indian Student Place-ment Service, under which Indian children nine years and older could, with their parents' consent, go away on buses to the homes of white families where they would be accepted and treated as family members. They would go to school. Hawk in Flight must go.

Again April Star had walked out into the desert early in the morning. Her struggle to let him go had been a cruel one. How could she send her only son away to a strange mother she did not know and into a home she had never seen? She was afraid for him. His spirit needed kindness, his words needed a listening ear. She would learn to read and write. She would teach Hawk in Flight. She would keep him with her. Then she remembered the young men in the town, and she knelt on the desert floor, a solitary figure, face toward heaven, and asked Heavenly Father to give her strength to send her son away. When she arose, there were tears on her face and determination in her heart.

Now, after nearly ten months, Hawk in Flight was coming home. The truck stopped. Her husband helped her down. She stood with the little group of parents, looking down the dirt road to where the yellow bus would appear.

Meantime Hawk in Flight was impatient with the slow pace of the school bus. He felt like two people — the brown Indian boy, free as the summer wind, and the awkward, scared little boy whose bewildered heart knew that his foster mother was just tolerating him, that she did not really love him.

His white mother had studied with him for an hour each day. She was determined that he should learn. She tried to mask her impatience. When she spoke angrily, he retreated further into his misery. His white brother, the same age as he, answered the questions easily.

Some days Hawk in Flight wished he could fly like the bird of his name; then he would fly back to the hogan with the dirt floor and the sheep pelt for a bed and to his beautiful, brown, quiet mother.

He often longed to be home, to take off his shirt and his stiff, hard shoes and run through the rocks and salt grass on the hillside where he had tended the sheep. It made him happy to remember the feel of the hot wind on his long hair. Now his hair was short and bristly. He was brother to the porcupine.

A great many things were frightening to him. The house of his white parents had many rooms. At first he had trembled in fear that he might stumble into a room he should not go. He knew chairs and tables, but he had never lived with them. He either sat too stiffly in a chair or slumped, trying to hide. Both were wrong. The daily bath was agonizing. The soap caused his skin to itch. He did not understand why clean clothes were necessary every day. The language was strange, and his mind had to translate many of the words into Indian meanings before he understood them.

His name was now Jimmy. He did not always respond to his white name; the sound was strange to his ears. Because he did not always respond, his white mother and his teachers thought he was slow. Young as he was, he knew this was not true, but some days he despaired of anybody in the white world discovering it. He was often frightened and miserable because he did not know what was expected of him. The white man's customs were strange. The food was different and caused his stomach to ache, but he did not speak of it. The knives and forks and spoons were not easy to use. He was not supposed to withdraw, and he was not allowed to be forward. Some days he felt suspended between two worlds; he did not seem to belong in either.

When Hawk in Flight went to Primary and Sunday School, he found that the white boys were sometimes noisy and boisterous. When he acted as they did, he was told he was naughty and disrespectful. The white children often teased or shunned him. He felt bewildered and angry. Once he struck back at a boy who made him miserable by tripping and pinching him. He was blamed. When the girls giggled and pointed at him, he felt hostile.

He thought often of his mother, April Star, and longed to sit and watch her as she wove rugs in intricate designs with colorful yarn she had dyed herself.

When the winter came, the unaccustomed cold made him uncomfortable. Even his new red coat did not keep him warm. Sometimes he would try to imagine the hot desert sun on his shoulders. When spring came, he thought of the sunset at home turning the whole desert pink, then red, then purple. He felt the urge to fly like the wind into that distant sunset.

Finally, the school year was over. He was excited to see his Indian friends who were waiting in the bus, but he was quiet on the ride home. He felt that his heart would burst with impatience. He wanted to see his family — his sisters, his grandmother, his silent father, and especially his mother. He imagined his mother waiting for him in her long, worn purple skirt and her high laced boots, her black hair braided, smooth and shiny, a leather thong holding it high off her shoulders. She would not say very much, but she would be glad to see him.

When he felt hungry, he realized it would be strange to eat with his hands again.

His thoughts went again to his white family. He knew that the beautiful, tense white mother did not want him to come back. He had not adjusted. *Adjusted* was a word that frightened him. He loved his Indian placement worker, but he did not always understand. What did it mean "to adjust"? He felt that that word threatened all his dreams and the dreams of his mother, April Star.

Yet he had new, exciting thoughts in his mind. He could read many things, and he could write. He had discovered that there were worlds hiding inside books. He reached for the books he was bringing home. He rubbed the covers longingly. He knew in his little-boy mind that he would go back to the white man's school somewhere. His stomach fluttered like a new bird about to leave its nest.

April Star saw him as he stepped off the bus. She knew he was troubled. She waited. They looked into each other's eyes. The communication between them was the same.

During the summer she knew that Hawk in Flight would not be one of the fortunate ones to go back into the same white home that fall. Peace, however, came to her through prayer. She felt that the Lord would direct those in charge to place him with a mother who would understand and love him. "I will write to her," she said to herself. While Hawk in Flight was away to school, the missionaries had taught her to read a little and write simple words. "I will tell her that Hawk in Flight is one of God's special sons."

Since then the years have sped by. Hawk in Flight has graduated from Brigham Young University. He holds a responsible position with an engineering firm in a city far away from the hogan. He teaches the Gospel Doctrine class in Sunday School.

April Star never tires of bearing her testimony. She says: "I look out of the window of the little house Hawk in Flight built for me next to the hogan. Silently I talk to Heavenly Father: 'The gospel of thy Son gave my son opportunity to learn, to be free. His white parents taught him the dream of a college education. I am glad. As swift and straight as the bird of his name, he pursued his dream. Now he is many thousands of miles away. I hope to see him at his desk someday.'

"The day my courage grew strong and I sent Hawk in Flight away to the Indian Student Placement Service, the Lord gave him wings to fly."

Our Peripheral Vision

And if thou draw out thy soul to the hungry, and satisfy the afflicted soul; then shall thy light rise in obscurity, and thy darkness be as the noonday:

And the Lord shall guide thee continually, and satisfy thy soul in drought, and make fat thy bones: and thou shalt be like a watered garden, and like a spring of water, whose waters fail not.

— Isaiah

11   "Look, Somebody! Here I Am!"

I sat in the waiting room of the mental hospital. The love I felt for Matt and the need to help him get off drugs and discover the scope of his potential overwhelmed me.

Sometimes it takes a number of people, people who are willing to give a gift of love in terms of time, prayers, and pleading, before another person comes to recognize his divine destiny. Matt was one of those.

I felt angry and disconsolate as I parked my car and walked up the steps of the state mental hospital. I had come to visit Matt — Matt, who at barely seventeen years of age had abdicated from the realities of life. He was on drugs, and at that time we had no other drug treatment facility but the state mental hospital.

It was I who had taken Matt there. Only two weeks earlier, at three o'clock on a Sunday morning, I had been awakened by a telephone call from a drug crisis center. They were calling with the news that a young man whom I had met when I participated in a community drug prevention seminar was threatening to commit suicide. He was asking for me.

"Dear God," I had prayed when I put the phone down, "please bless him to respond to something, to somebody, before he destroys his health and his splendid intellect. Help him awaken to his exceptional capabilities and to fulfill his potential."

Matt was a pathetic figure when I reached him. He was sitting in the gutter, his thin, gaunt body bent over, his head nearly touching the ground. His long gangly legs were doubled under him.

As my heart went out to him, I remembered a typewritten poem handed to me some time previously by an official at the Salt Lake County Detention Home. It had been written by a fourteen-year-old girl who was institutionalized. She lay curled in the fetal position, hopelessly sleeping mortal life away. She resisted even momentary awakening to the challenging, beautiful, yet sometimes terrifying world in which we all must live. In her poem she had uncannily identified and verbalized the need of lost and lonely souls — like Matt.

AN APPEAL

Here I am
    LOOK
Eyes and mouth and bone like anyone
And with a soul like anyone
And with a heart like anyone
    that beats fast
Yet
    No one sees me or
        they look and look away and go away
          and I sleep inside.
It is a deep sleep with no friends to dream about
    and no enemies
      and nobody.
If I could smile and you would smile back with
    your eyes —
If I could touch your wrist and you would lead me —
    I would wake up then.
But somehow I cannot smile or touch or whisper
I don't know why
    I don't know.
   Somebody tell me why.
    Hello, somebody.
Here I am
    LOOK

Matt had been "shot up" on speed for eight days. I found him some food. He had no stomach for it, but I urged him to eat. Food would help him come off his high. He needed to talk.

He had been once to the mental hospital for the "cure." Now

the juvenile judge had given him a choice — the reform school for wayward youths, where there was little or no help for drug abusers beyond incarceration, or back to the mental hospital. Through clenched teeth and with tears running down his face he said he'd kill himself before he went back to the hospital. He was scheduled to appear in court the next morning. We found a quiet spot, on the side of a hill overlooking the valley, where we could talk.

Matt told me he had been born and raised in an affluent family, the third of eight children. He wasn't placing the blame for his drug addiction on his parents, but it kept coming through that his brother, just sixteen months older than he, was a model son. He went on and on about how great his brother was. His near-perfect older brother seemed to represent some self-respectability in Matt which I might miss if he didn't emphasize it. I felt that he'd been unfavorably compared to his brother. Without verbalizing it, Matt revealed that he had always been lonely and had repeatedly cried out: "Look, somebody! Here I am!"

He told me of an experience he had had at Primary when he was nine years old. His teacher had told the class that Elder Spencer W. Kimball had read the Book of Mormon, from cover to cover, when he was nine years old. She challenged the class to read it. Matt struggled through every word of it alone, then he started reading the Doctrine and Covenants. When he proudly reported his accomplishments to his Primary class, some of the kids laughed. He retreated into himself once again, a friendless, lonely little boy. As he grew older, he began looking for acceptance elsewhere.

When Matt entered junior high school, he made friends with kids from what he called the "Street." "Street" kids formed a fraternity of sorts, a place for lost, lonely kids who were desperately seeking acceptance. Drugs were a part of the brotherhood. He began staying away from home for days at a time.

I listened, and Matt talked on. His story was not new. Sometimes he would say something for its shock value, and out of the corner of his eye he would watch my reaction. When he did that, I would simply say, "Matt, I love you — I care about you." Finally, he talked himself out. We sat silent in the bright sunlight. After a little while he asked me why I loved him. My heart flooded with gratitude. He didn't say, "Do you really love me?"; or, "How can you love me?"; but "Why?"

I did love him. Love had worked its miracle.

"Suppose," I said, "just suppose, Matt, that you and I were friends before we came to this earth. Suppose that one day I said to you: 'I'm going on ahead of you. If we should meet in earth life, what do you see at this point in time as the thing you would want me to do for you?' If we suppose that such a conversation took place, what do you think your answer would have been?"

He began to cry. I sat in silence, waiting. After while he said, "You wouldn't believe it if I told you."

"Yes, I would," I said.

"Well" — the words came falteringly — "I would have said, 'Help me to practice godhood.' "

I had no words — only tears. A skinny, seventeen-year-old kid who had broken the law of the land as well as the moral law, who was destroying his body, putting his mind in jeopardy, and dulling the voice of the Holy Spirit with drugs — he was still wanting to claim a dream given by Father; a possibility of godhood.

I had an overwhelming feeling of how precious Matt was to the Lord.

We talked about our divine parentage. "You know," he said, "I've sung 'I Am a Child of God' since I was little, but I've never really assented to being his child until now." His face held a kind of wonder.

I asked, "Matt, who do you think would have said the last good-bye to you as you left your heavenly home?"

He thought about it. "Mother in heaven," he said.

"What do you think she would have said to you?"

His blue eyes looked straight into mine. "She would have said, 'Come home to me.' " I took his hand. Again we wept; this time together.

The next morning I went with him into the judge's chambers, where he was sentenced to an indefinite stay at the mental hospital. As I drove him to the hospital he was subdued and quiet. It was not easy for him to return, but before leaving me in the very anteroom where I now sat waiting to see him, he had committed himself to do his best. He had turned as the attendant led him away. "Come to see me," he said. Then, falteringly, "I love you — too!"

These former scenes had flashed before me and I was remembering the forlorn look in Matt's eyes the day he was committed, when a voice startled me: "Please sign in — I'll show you where to go."

Matt was living in a men's ward — a boy of seventeen years, living with men sick in mind and spirit who had committed all manner of degrading acts. One of them, Matt told me, was a murderer.

I had brought him some records, since he delighted in classical music — Beethoven, Brahms, Bach. He showed me his room. His optimism heartened me. He was, in his words, "shaping up."

I visited him at the mental hospital as often as I could. Three months later he was released.

I wish I could say that his struggle was over, but it wasn't. He tried to join the army. He was too young. He dropped out of school again and went back on the "Street." I saw him often. He would commit himself to try, but he didn't seem to really believe he had the strength.

We went to a movie together on his eighteenth birthday. The next day he borrowed his sister's car to take a boyfriend to his home in another state. The boy stashed drugs in the car. The boys were picked up for speeding and the drugs were found. Matt was sentenced to a year in the state penitentiary. He was now too far away for me to visit.

Matt did his best to gain from that experience. He studied and passed his high school equivalency test. During the last three months of his sentence he was allowed to go to a junior college in another town. He spent the night in jail and went to school during the day. He met a lovely girl in his sociology class. They became good friends. When she saw that Matt was becoming serious about her, she told him that she was waiting for her missionary sweetheart.

Each student in the sociology class was assigned a field project. Hers was to interview a number of inmates at the jail. She was shocked to find Matt there.

That precious young woman somehow "brought it all together" for Matt. Shocked as she was, she did not turn away from him. She talked to him about his priesthood and shared with him the experiences of her missionary. She bore her testimony and told him she would always care about him — as a spirit brother. She asked him to let her bishop visit him.

Matt began to pray again and to study the scriptures. When he was released, he went back home and enrolled in the university.

"I married the library," he said. "The 'good' kids didn't want me, and I didn't want to associate with my former 'Street friends'." He studied so hard that he made the dean's honor list. He took several institute classes. He was determined to spend as much time studying the gospel as he spent on his scholastic studies.

Matt became active in his ward. He still felt unaccepted there, but it didn't matter any more.

One lovely spring evening he came to tell me that he had received a mission call. He said that he had been to the temple often in the previous six weeks. "I don't know if you know," he said, "but my parents' divorce became final today. There was a time when I couldn't have handled this, but I have spent the whole day in the temple. I am at peace."

Two years later, by appointment, our doorbell rang. Matt stood there, smiling, tall, straight, and handsome — a boy grown to the stature of a man. He bore testimony of the Lord Jesus Christ. "I'm ready to do some volunteer work," he said, "but I'd rather not work with people on drugs." It was said with humility born of wisdom.

Matt has since been married in the temple. He and his lovely wife have been blessed with a beautiful baby boy. Now there are two people who depend on him — two people to whom he is of prime importance. He has accepted his responsibilities. He is giving. He is needed. He is loved. He has, at last, found his place. He belongs.

12 This Day Has Salvation Come to Your House

President Spencer W. Kimball has said: "As the contrasts between the ways of the world and the ways of God become sharpened by circumstance, the faith of the members of the Church will be tried even more severely. One of the most vital things we can do is to express our testimonies through service, which will, in turn, produce spiritual growth, greater commitment, and a greater capacity to keep the commandments." (Ensign, December 1974, page 5.)

The volunteer experiences of the people in this chapter demonstrate service in action. By such accounts, those who know they should be giving their time and talents to a worthy cause will perhaps be motivated to take the advice of a little motto that President Spencer W. Kimball keeps on his desk: "Do It."

Ned Vincent spends one night a week answering the telephone for a crisis line. He is deeply committed to being available to people in trouble. One night a distraught woman called. She told him that she was depressed and had decided to commit suicide.

Ned felt that all his training and experience was on the line. He talked to her quietly and caringly while he dialed the number of another volunteer, who stood by on the phone until Ned could get the address of the caller. Then he told her that someone would be there soon to help her. She was incredulous.

Ned found it difficult to convince her that there were two people in the world who really cared about her.

It was a delicate situation. If he said the wrong thing or used the wrong tone of voice she might hang up and be out of reach of help. He prayed. The thought came that maybe she had a child. He felt so strongly about it that he asked, "How is your daughter?"

There was a long silence. He was afraid he had lost contact, and he almost panicked. Then the caller began to weep. "How did you know I have a daughter?" she asked. "Tell me about her," Ned replied.

Now the woman began to cry and to talk about her daughter, who was in a distant state. It was twenty-five minutes before Ned heard her doorbell ring, and he knew that the volunteer he had called had arrived. It took Ned another five minutes to give the woman courage enough to answer the door. He had saved a life.

Spencer Call is a pediatrician. He has been in practice for years. Every Wednesday he spends eight hours at a free clinic giving his gift of love and professional training. "Why do you give your time and service without charge?" he was asked by a colleague. "Some of those doctors at the clinic are paid."

"If I wanted to be paid in *money*," replied Dr. Call, "I'd get an extra job or spend the day in my own office."

A well-known psychiatrist gives six weeks of volunteer service each year to the patients in a mental institution. He comes back to his own practice refreshed, brimming with new ideas and new commitment.

The Brunson family — father, mother, and six children —

decided to spend a day cleaning up the yard of a lonely widow. It was hard work, and the widow Johnson didn't seem too grateful. When it was over, Bud Brunson gathered his children around him. "Lots of people have pulled weeds in Mrs. Johnson's yard and picked up the trash and bagged it," he said, "but they've gone away afterwards and forgotten her. They did their good deed to make themselves feel good. Let's do our good deed to make Mrs. Johnson happy. Let's not go straight home; let's go in and visit for a while. Then let's visit her at least monthly."

And they do.

A group of young people painted old Dan Watson's house and barn. It was a worthy service project, but they didn't just wash out their paint brushes, pick up their ladder, and walk out of Mr. Watson's life. They committed themselves that one by one they would drop by Mr. Watson's house each week; nineteen young people pledged that for nineteen weeks one of them would listen to an old man who needed to reminisce and give advice and in the process learn something from and about the new generation. The visits proved to be more Christlike than painting the house and barn — though that too was needed.

President Harold B. Lee blessed and encouraged volunteering when he said:

> We fervently thank the Lord for the faithfulness and devotion of many in and out of the Church who are in high places in business, in governmental circles, in the legal profession, doctors, trained social workers, nurses, and those in the fields of the sciences and the arts. Particularly are we grateful for those who accept positions of leadership in the Church, who serve as home teachers or class leaders in the priesthood or in the auxiliaries, who make themselves available for volunteer service in helping to care for the unfortunate in all lands and among minorities within and without the Church, and in giving particular attention to the needs of the widows and the orphans.
>
> I say to all such, as did Jesus to Zacchaeus: "This day is salvation come to [their] house." (Luke 19:9.) These are they who are holding fast to

the "iron rod" which can lead us all, in safety, to the tree of life. (*Ensign*, June 1971, page 9.)

And what is the iron rod? In answer to his brothers' questions, Nephi explained it:

> And they said unto me: What meaneth the rod of iron which our father saw, that led to the tree?
>
> And I said unto them that it was the word of God; and whoso would hearken unto the word of God, and would hold fast unto it, they would never perish; neither could the temptations and the fiery darts of the adversary overpower them unto blindness, to lead them away to destruction. (1 Nephi 15:23-24.)

What a glorious promise to those who so sincerely desire to know Jesus that they make themselves available to him, ever ready to hear and heed the call to serve!

13 Where Have All the Good Guys Gone?

The decency, graciousness, and generosity of the everyday giver is not always known. Bob's "Do It" list helps us realize how much each one of us really does give and how we receive each day numerous gifts of love from unpretentious givers.

Bob, a successful and busy businessman, is an everyday giver. After business hours he can usually be found in his shop or at a friend's or neighbor's doing an intricate repair job. He is gifted and clever. He makes a tiny sailboat for a grandchild or neighbor boy with the same pride and enthusiasm as he has in building a fine piece of furniture. He's the proverbial do-it man. He can fix the leaky plumbing, repair the electric stove, mend a precious piece of china, remodel a bathroom, and pay the bills.

His wife believes he can do anything. When he changed the window in the family room from an insignificant one to a beautiful picture window, she exclaimed: "You've brought the mountain right into our home. Now you're moving mountains! How would you like to make the drapes?" She believes he could do it, too.

It's fun to read his "To-Do" list:

Fix Reed's lock
Prune Grant's bushes
Repair Jack's garage door
Sister Johnson needs a new door
The Joneses need help laying some turf

Give Mary Lou some suggestions on her remodeling
Make Jason a car for the midget Derby
Build Robert a chest for his bridles and riding gear
Frame Rian's painting
Build some fruit room shelves for the Smiths, Palmers,
    and Lees
Repair Brad's carburetor
Fertilize Jamison's lawn

There are always many people who need to know where to get the best price when they want to buy a new car, a television, a tub, a light fixture, or a trailer. Bob will go out of his way to help them, spending hours running down leads and making arrangements. He delivers, too.

People confide in Bob. He gives them of his wisdom and offers his heart. By that I mean that he readily says: "I love you. You're like a brother to me. You're great!" He spends a few hours each week on the phone, keeping in touch with loved relatives and friends. He's a great visitor, too. He keeps track of people — he doesn't walk out of their lives as the years bring new circumstances and new responsibilities.

Yes, Bob is a giver. He's willing to see what is needed and ready to do it. And he is one of the happiest people I know.

No doubt you know at least one Bob — those wonderful, unselfish people who would be startled if you identified their giving as "good works."

"Where have all the good guys gone?" They're all around us. Perhaps you're one of them.

I WONDER

What would happen if each drop
Of rain refused to fall,
Or every sunbeam ceased to shine
Because it was so small?

What would happen if each day
We chose to leave undone
An act of kindness just because
It was a little one?

— Esther F. Thomas

14 Love Comes Naturally

It's as natural for Craig to give as it is for him to breathe. He doesn't wait for structured opportunities but scatters seeds of love as prolifically as Johnny Appleseed planted apple trees.

When asked how he accomplishes miracles, Craig laughed and said, "Miracles belong to God." But Craig is one of God's instruments.

Craig has an uncanny ability to identify the confused and the lonely. It is as though he has a divining rod within that alerts him to people's hidden hurts. I've known him to step up to strangers and initiate happy, uplifting conversations. "Here, let me help you with that" is so warmly said that when the person addressed looks into his face there is a silent salute from one to the other. Most of us don't take the time to experience such special spirit-to-spirit communication. Yet it's the "people touch" that keeps us striving to achieve, that lifts us above life's discouragements and dilemmas.

Ned and his father moved into our ward when Ned was about ten. News soon got around that Ned's mother had abandoned them. As a result, Ned couldn't believe he was worthy of anybody's love. He seldom lifted his eyes, and he spoke with a stammer.

Ned's peers felt his insecurity and cruelly used it against him. They made his life miserable until Craig noticed him.

Craig was seventeen that spring. It was heartwarming to see him give that little fellow just what he needed to lift his self-esteem. Craig took him fishing, taught him the mystique of discovering when the fish were feeding, and showed him how to secure one to his hook and net it.

Once Craig fell into the water, and Ned laughed until he fell in too. They just sat in the water and laughed at each other. One day I saw them sitting on the bank of a stream, talking earnestly as Craig taught Ned the art of tying flies. Later that summer Craig discovered that Ned had a natural bent for baseball; so he coached the boy. He demanded a lot of Ned. Craig went with Ned when he tried out for Little League and won the catcher's position. Ned surprised the other kids and their dads. He was a talented little ballplayer. His catcher's mitt seemed to give him confidence, and the kids cheered for him. And all the time Craig never abdicated his self-appointed responsibility. He loved Ned and Ned knew it.

I couldn't say exactly when Ned began to look people directly in the eye; to my knowledge, however, Ned never stammered again after that summer. He became a confident young man, happy and self-assured.

When asked how he accomplished that miracle, Craig laughed and said, "Miracles belong to God."

Teenagers are Craig's special target. He senses when they feel hurt or lonely. He recognizes the symptoms of disillusionment and mistrust. He helps without coming on too heavy. He "stays in there" and sticks like a cocklebur until he finds the key to their hearts.

"Craig," I said one day, "are you ever rebuffed?" He looked startled, then laughed. "What's a rebuff? At least it's a reaction — an interchange, and that's what's needed at times."

Craig has a talent for giving himself away; not in bits and pieces, but completely.

15 A Quest for Peace

To be dedicated to being our brother's keeper is not always rewarding and comfortable for the giver. The giver frequently experiences soul-searching and suffering because of the other person's inability to care consistently enough to see the need for change even when he is on the brink of disaster. It takes courage to stand by with assurances and reassurances of love while another heaps up sorrow for himself. It requires patience, perception, and precision in timing to know when he's ready for help. To give when another is open to receive often means sacrifice and inconvenience. The committed helper is not always having a good time, but he knows when to disregard his own personal needs and, in sickness or health, rise to the occasion.

A sincere giver comes to see that, "in the eyes of God, no man is crippled or blind except in his own soul...."

Yet the giver is not always successful; he doesn't always give another faith in himself, or turn his steps to walk in the light. In the following account, Melissa is like the girl who prays "Lord, make me good, but not now!"

It is difficult to capture on the written page the fragility of Melissa's soul, as she suffers from the laceration of disbelieving that the Lord can ever truly love her. The death of a loved one with its irreversible finality is not the same. To sit helplessly by the bedside of a child, parent, spouse, or beloved friend who is too ill to respond, is still another dimension of suffering.

The immense chasm Melissa has found that she must bridge between the actuality of her "now" life style and the terrible need for some reality, however infinitesimal, that Heavenly Father still loves her is staggering.

Ten years ago Melissa joined the Church. She is now twenty-two. She is intelligent, scholarly, and creative. She came to classify herself as an intellectual Mormon and aligned herself with baptized Church members who negate the spiritual and worship intellectually, haughtily proud of their ability to think and reason. She couldn't understand that she could approach the gospel both intellectually and spiritually.

She began to believe it an evidence of intellectual weakness to allow herself to experience spiritual needs. She backed herself into a corner. The light could come from one direction only. She now has found that an intellectual acceptance of the gospel, without faith in the Lord Jesus Christ, is empty, and that the life-giving, life-guiding force of the gospel is many-faceted.

Melissa became a proponent of a women's liberation movement. She allowed herself to be deceived by the positive aspects of equality of women. She did not realize that women are equal to men. "Liberation," she was to find, cannot make men and women the same — it depersonalizes both in its attempt to make them the same. She came to know that any loss of the sacredness of the individual, man or woman, is not of the Lord and defeats peace and happiness — the very purpose of life.

Melissa became a disciple of the old-new cult of confusion, inappropriately and untruthfully labeled — "love"; that self-robbing philosophy that says we must give and share anything we have; that we must supposedly care so deeply about another and his physical, philosophical, and emotional needs that to supply them we will sacrifice on the altar of "do your own thing" even our own inner knowledge of what is right. Thus she found herself caught up in the counterfeit of the heaven-blessed marriage relationship. She settled for "with all my earthly goods I thee endow, including my body and brain," without benefit of clergy or state.

For a period of time she would not admit that she had spiritual needs, yet those needs were so deep that, as bizarre as her life had become, they kept surfacing.

One morning she awakened knowing she was not a liberated woman and never would be. She was not self-sufficient. She did not have her life in control. Everyone in her "home" looked to her for strength. They thought she had it all straight. The effort of keeping a smooth, false face had become debilitating.

After nights of anguish she did what she knew she must do — she went to see her bishop. What the bishop did for her was specific, beautiful, and Christlike. It came to him as the result of prayer.

The bishop did not zero in on her mistakes. He was already conversant with much of the story she poured out to him. He knew she was still in the drug scene with marijuana. He had felt grave concern over her living arrangement, but she had resisted giving him the opportunity to talk about it. She now told him she was living in a commune, but though he recognized the negative implications, he did not preach, moralize, or condemn.

The bishop quietly asked her, in her own words, "to do two piddlin' little things": to pray daily and to read the scriptures for at least ten minutes each day. He told her that her prayers would become more effectual if she would pray in specifics. She tried, and there gradually came into her life "a little circle of emotional peace." "It isn't much," she commented, "but it's all I've got."

"Since talking to the bishop, I've been staying with a girl friend. I haven't leveled with Tom — he's the fellow I've been living with. I just haven't gone home. When you've invested your whole self in a person, you can't walk off as though nothing ever happened. I have that ahead of me.

"I know I can never be where marijuana is used. I have an emotional dependency on marijuana.

"I realize I'm building some kind of substructure, some small base on which I can build a foundation. When I have a solid place to stand, I can begin to build toward complete repentance. I'm not sure I can hold on, nor hold out for the whole deal, but I know that without the Lord's help I'm inextricable. When I feel peace I can hold on another hour — another day. In the back of my mind is the hope that one of these hours I will come to know that the Savior's atoning power can be efficacious for me. I know the prayer of David — I wish I could have faith in it.

> Out of the depths have I cried unto thee, O Lord.
>
> Lord, hear my voice: let thine ears be attentive to the voice of my supplications.
>
> If thou, Lord, shouldest mark iniquities, O Lord, who shall stand? (Psalm 130:1-3.)

I don't think of this prayer often, though, because my hold on emotional peace and closeness with the Lord is so precarious that I may let go at any one of these minutes I'm trying to live through. I'm fragile and cut up inside, but I've come to know that closeness with the Lord is something I must have to live at all."

After Melissa's interview with the bishop, she flew hundreds of miles to meet with one who loves her unconditionally, one who prays for her and pleads and suffers with her. She needed to be listened to and to be reinforced with that unjudgmental love. She needed another's testimony that through repentance she could still qualify for all the blessings that the Father has in store for "those that love him and keep his commandments."

> ... The joy and suffering of those we love are part of our own existence. We feel their triumphs and defeats, their hopes and fears, their anger and pity, and our lives are richer for it. ... Love and friendship dissolve the rigidities of the isolated self, force new perspectives, alter judgments and keep in working order the emotional substratum on which all profound comprehension of human affairs must rest. (John W. Gardner, *Self-Renewal* [New York: Harper and Row, 1965], page 16.)

Because of Melissa's compliance with the specific things

the bishop asked her to do — pray, and read the scriptures ten minutes a day — apparently she is approaching the point of ridding herself of the burden of mistakes and sins that are too heavy for her to bear. She has been disfellowshipped from the Church. If she really desires to she can now lay all her burdens at the feet of the Savior and begin anew.

She is being buffeted by Satan. Life is not easy for her. Each day brings its heartache and suffering. She sometimes finds herself doubting her sanity. Melissa must walk through the low valley and climb her own mountain.

Her friend can only stay close, verbalize her love, and be available. Not long ago she sent Melissa a note. It contained three verses of scripture:

> Come unto me, all ye that labour and are heavy laden, and I will give you rest.

> Take my yoke upon you, and learn of me; for I am meek and lowly in heart: and ye shall find rest unto your souls.

> For my yoke is easy, and my burden is light. (Matthew 11:28-30.)

Those who love and give cannot always claim success; but in making the effort they move a little closer to understanding that if they desire to share the Savior's burden they cannot avoid suffering.

16 Hung Up on Hang-Ups

"Be not forgetful to entertain strangers: for thereby some have entertained angels unawares." (Hebrews 13:2.)

Not everyone cares deeply enough about his spirit brothers and sisters to be sensitive to their needs. Some are trapped by their own "hang-ups." They apply layers of "patching plaster" that temporarily protect but do not allow wounds to heal.

"Hang-ups" needn't turn into "hold-ups," robbing the person of growth and progression. If he will only break down the walls of resistance by giving of himself, his "hang-ups" can become opportunities to exercise humility and to seek the Lord with new-found courage.

Patti labels herself "the original hang-up girl." She has keen insight into the problems which held up her progress and happiness for twelve years.

"On the surface," she says, "our life looked as normal as most of our friends. We had a nice home, four healthy children, and my husband had a fairly good job that provided the necessities and a few luxuries.

"Yet most of the time I was difficult to live with. I nearly lost my husband's respect and confidence. I was a disappointment to him. I was not keeping stride with him spiritually. As I look back, I realize I wasn't even going in the same direction he was, and I didn't much care. He was alternately patient and impatient, but deeply hurt. It showed in his face and in the way he handled me with the proverbial 'kid gloves.'

"We were married in the temple and he wanted to make our marriage eternal. He kept telling me that he loved me and that he wanted us to be together always. I wasn't listening. I didn't have a testimony of eternal marriage or of the gospel of Jesus Christ. I didn't care to be active, but at Gary's insistence I went along with him to meetings.

"When Gary paid tithing and other Church financial obligations, I was unpleasant for days. Thank goodness he had the backbone to disregard my hostility.

"I could weep now over the obstacles I placed in his way when he was called to be second counselor in the bishopric."

To the inquiry of how she came to recognize herself as a "hang-up girl," she replies: "Gary was usually surrounded by people with problems and heartaches. He patiently tried to explain his motive, but I could only see the time and energy people took that I selfishly felt belonged to me.

"One night at about 10:30 the doorbell rang. Gary, as usual, was attending a meeting. There on the doorstep stood a little fifteen-year-old girl. She was crying. Usually I would have said, 'Brother Robins isn't home,' and closed the door, but she struck a responsive chord deep inside me; memories flashed through my mind that I thought were safely dead and buried. I invited her in, and she literally fell into my arms. I held her and began crying with her.

"After a while, I led her into the family room and we talked for hours. I became conscious of the little, love-deprived girl within me, waiting like a wraith to be released. My heart defrosted as I comforted Jayne, and the little girl inside me grew up. I realized that I had suffered hardening of the heart because I had believed that no one could hurt as deeply as I hurt. My mother had died when I was five, and my father simply disappeared. An aunt and uncle took me in. I was not physically abused, but the emotional bruises to which I was subjected daily had never really healed. I wouldn't listen to anyone's problems; I wouldn't let myself care enough to help anybody. I rationalized that if people had problems it was probably their own fault, so they could just help themselves. I, who had more 'hang-ups' than I could count, had taken a self-righteous attitude toward others. I now feel aghast at my own audacity.

"I didn't know when Gary came home that night, but wisely he did not interrupt us.

"Jayne's mother had died three years previously, leaving her, an only child, in the care of an alcoholic father. She had lived with five different relatives in three years. She was constantly reminded of how kind they were for allowing her room and board, so rightfully 'she should work for it.' She did.

"About the time that she would adjust somewhat to the household where she was living, her father would show up and drag her to the home of another relative. Most of the time he would leave her on the doorstep, a forlorn, bewildered, weeping child, feeling shame and fright.

"If she was living with her mother's relatives, they would tell her how careful she must be not to turn out like her father. If she was living with her father's relatives, they would make a point of telling her that her mother had driven her father to drink.

"She wore clothing which was grudgingly contributed by her cousins, who made it a point to tell this to the kids at school. Her cousins expected her to thank them.

"These were only a few of the indignities Jayne had suffered. I knew them all, and then some. Later I made her a bed on the couch and called the relatives with whom she was living to tell them that Jayne was staying overnight with us. They hadn't even missed her.

"In the wee hours of the morning, I went to bed but not to sleep. I needed to talk with Gary. He was asleep, but I knew he was waiting for me — he'd waited a long, long time for the real me to surface. He had never lost faith. I believe he knew a change had been wrought in my heart before I said a word. I put my arms around him. The dam had broken at last. Gary was deluged with my tears and talk until the alarm clock went off. He reached over and turned it off. Simultaneously, we began to laugh. As he kissed me, I realized he had been crying too. Mine were tears of regret and of the need to be understood and forgiven for all the misery he'd endured — or rather *we'd* endured, because I had not been exactly happy, 'hung-up' as I was. Gary's tears were tears of gratitude, compassion, and love.

"We knelt close together in prayer, hands entwined, unified as we had never been before. As he prayed, the phrase 'a broken heart and a contrite spirit' kept repeating itself in my soul. I understood the meaning of those cleansing, sacred words.

"With the help of the bishop, Gary was able to talk Jayne's father into releasing her to us. We became Jayne's foster parents. Sixteen months later her father became gravely ill, and in remorse for neglecting Jayne he allowed us to adopt her legally. Before he died, Jayne built a friendly relationship with her father and felt to sincerely forgive him. I'm extremely grateful, for in so doing she let go of all the hurt and scarring she had suffered. For much longer I had carried my hurt inside me, where it had festered. I feel confident that this will never happen to Jayne.

"Jayne has been our daughter for three years.

"Last week Gary and I returned from a dinner party. Jayne was standing with her back to us, scrubbing the sink. The house was tidy, the younger children were in bed. Rock music was playing on the stereo. Her long auburn hair was flying back and forth, her shirt tail keeping time with the music. Jayne's bare legs and feet were brown below her rolled-up jeans. 'Hi,' Gary called, 'you look happy.'

"She turned towards us, her face radiant. 'I am,' she said.

"I stood smiling, silent, as she turned back to her work. But my heart cried out: 'Oh, Jayne, you are so grateful to us; you, who are supposedly the receiver, can never fully realize what you have given me. You set my feet on the road to exaltation and eternal life.' "

Our Panoramic Vision

Love is one of the chief characteristics of Deity, and ought to be manifested by those who aspire to be the sons of God. A man filled with the love of God, is not content with blessing his family alone, but ranges through the whole world, anxious to bless the whole human race.

— Joseph Smith

17 Charlie

Charlie Stewart knew that the gift is love. He gave it with spontaneous constancy. He knew that love must be given away to be possessed. He realized that when we serve one another we accept God's need for us to alleviate his children's suffering and sorrow. Charlie understood, as few people come to understand, that when we give love, one to another, we come to know and love God and ourselves. He wanted that for everyone – worldwide.

I knew Charlie Stewart had cancer. I went to see him one day at his office. He had been through an operation and rigorous therapy, but on that particular day he looked well and vigorous. His eyes held the old twinkle, but I noticed that he walked with a slight limp. We talked about the many new resources that were successfully helping people in trouble. I came away lifted and strengthened, grateful once again that the Lord had allowed me a beautiful friendship with my spirit brother.

Months later Charlie's condition worsened. He went back to the hospital for additional therapy. I happened to meet a mutual friend who told me how sick Charlie looked. I wrote him a note: "Dear Charlie, ... Is there something I can do for you? ..."

When Charlie was back at his desk he phoned and asked me to come in; there was something I could do. I was grateful to respond. For 2½ years I had the privilege of helping lift his burden. I was the one benefited.

Charlie was the director of the Volunteer Services for LDS Social Services. He had received a mandate to organize needed areas of services and to recruit and train volunteers to serve those in need. The program also offered training resources, when requested by priesthood leadership, to assist ward and stake personal welfare service committees give maximum help to those in their wards and stakes who had socioemotional needs.

Charlie Stewart's desire was to involve people in the process of strengthening their brothers and sisters. His vision encompassed the whole world of man — Church members and nonmembers. He realized that the actualization of the vision must begin within the Church — the gospel of Jesus Christ must be accepted and lived. This would make possible "the placing of all known resources for the benefit of man under priesthood direction, a legal administrator, that the needs of all could be met in the Lord's way." Charlie desired that all areas of service, pioneered, organized, and refined by the LDS Social Services Volunteer Program, eventually become the responsibility of ward and stake personal welfare service committees, enabling members to care for those in their own ecclesiastical units on a one-to-one basis.

"As the Saints' needs are met," Charlie said, "they will reach out to their neighbors, and soon the outward reach of love and service will encircle the whole world, preparing both giver and receiver for the day when ". . . the kingdom of God shall go forth, that the kingdom of heaven may come. . . ." (D&C 65:6.)

One day Charlie told me of the experience that resulted in his desire to spend his life in service to others.

As a young farm boy, still tender from his two-year mission of offering the gospel of Jesus Christ to the people of Australia, he found himself catapulted into the Korean War. His first assignment was to help police the numerous brothels and houses of prostitution in Pusan. His soul was wounded by the rawness of the sin and the suffering around him. He saw the frozen bodies of little children strewn along the streets. On nearly every corner were bundles of clothing, rotting. The dead children were the victims of a bureaucracy that could successfully collect clothing but could not cut the red tape that would allow the clothing to be distributed.

He wrote to his stake president, explained the situation, and asked that the people in his stake gather and send him warm, usable clothing. One month went by, and another. Suffering and death continued unalleviated. He felt an anxiety that he had not communicated the urgent need.

Then one day at mail call he was told there was a package for him. When he went to collect it, he found numerous packages, all containing clothing. He assembled all the LDS soldiers he could find, and they began the task of sorting the clothing according to sizes. A tough sergeant, not a member of the Church, whose profane language was a cover-up for a tender heart, realized they would need a truck to distribute the clothing. He commandeered a truck, and the clothing was distributed to orphanages and institutions for the homeless.

The following account is from the newspaper of the navy base at Pusan:

EX-MISSIONARY CONTINUES TO HELP NEEDY PERSONS BY RECEIVING AID FOR KOREANS

PFC Charlie Stewart, a pleasant, soft-spoken, likable young man from Meadow, Utah, is living proof that Military Policemen have a heart.

Stewart, currently serving with the 563rd MP Co., has taken upon himself the task of providing some Christmas cheer for the many orphaned and under-privileged Korean children in this area. As a result of his pleas to the folks back home on behalf of these innocent victims of war, Stewart has amassed thirty-five [later they numbered one hundred] large packages of clothing and other necessary items. They formed so large a heap that special storage had to be provided for them in the company supply room, and they are still coming in!

This isn't the first time that Stewart has devoted his time to a cause he believes in. Prior to his induction into the army, while he was still a college student, he was called upon by The Church of Jesus Christ of Latter-day Saints (Mormons), of which he is a member, to serve as a missionary in Australia. He promptly ditched his college career and spent the next two years in many of the more remote areas of that continent, helping these people he served and preaching his religion.

Stewart hasn't yet decided how he will distribute his many gifts which have been sent mostly by the women's Relief Society of his church. But he has been discussing the question with the Mormon chaplain at the Korean Base Section Chapel and with Chaplain (Maj.) D. Helm, 91st Chaplain.

One thing is certain. Because of his kindness, there will be a great number of warm, happy kids who might otherwise have a difficult time this winter.

Stewart is unmarried and plans to return to college under the GI bill, to major in Sociology after he has completed his tour of duty.

Charlie was honored with five military awards: The National Defense Service Medal, Republic of Korea Presidental Unit Service Citation, the Meritorious Unit Commendation, the United Nations Service Medal, and the Bronze Star.

That experience changed the direction of Charlie's life.

As a child, he was extremely shy. A physical deformity of his lower jaw caused a speech impediment that required several operations to correct and made him self-conscious and retiring. He avoided social relationships in his peer-group. He shunned experiences that focused attention on him.

His mission experience had brought growth and some confidence in these areas, but he still felt uncomfortable in situations that required him to be with groups of people. It took considerable determination and conviction to commit his life to service for others.

When his tour of duty in Korea was over, he put away his dreams and desires to go back to the peace and security of the little farm in Meadow, Utah, and returned to college. He became a social worker with an advanced degree that opened doors for him to spend his lifetime effectively helping others. He yearned to walk always with the Savior. He understood the meaning of the words, "Verily I say unto you, Inasmuch as ye have done it unto one of the least of these my brethren, ye have done it unto me." (Matthew 25:40.)

Nineteen years later it was discovered that Charlie had

cancer of the spine. He requested that his high priests group leader administer to him. As the group leader did so, he received the distinct impression that only if the power of the priesthood was exercised in his behalf would Charlie be privileged to live and accomplish the great mission that would benefit many thousands of people, for the adversary desired to thwart his work. He returned home and called each high priest in the group and invited him to participate in a three-day fast so that they might have the humility, the strength, and the power to rebuke the disease.

After the fast, the high priests group leader again administered to Charlie, and he felt the assurance, through the Spirit, that the Lord desired Charlie to remain upon the earth until his work was finished.

For five years Charlie Stewart lived on the brink of eternity. Yet he lived life more abundantly than most. His whole being responded in appreciation and sensitivity to people, whoever they were, whatever their circumstances. He loved with a non-judgmental love. He had the capacity to assess needs and to see mistakes and sins, but he never labeled people as sinners. To him the breadth, depth, and height of joy and beauty, even his pain and suffering, were magnified by his acute awareness of life's expendability.

He often expressed an overwhelming gratefulness to Heavenly Father for the knowledge of the nature of his illness, because it motivated him to "be about his Father's business" with urgency and dedication.

He awakened many nights, cognizant of the Holy Spirit pouring inspiration into his keen mind and receptive heart. He recorded on cassette tape, plans for new programs, areas of service, and names of people who should be offered the privilege of being involved in giving one-to-one service.

Action initiating a service was not to be delayed. When his pain and suffering made it impossible for him to be mobile, he used the telephone. He asked people to come to him, gave them assignments and opportunities to serve.

During the last few months of his life, he taped and interviewed many givers and receivers of love through service, urging each to share deeply for the benefit of others. Some of the experiences recorded in this book are taken from those interviews.

During the last two weeks of his life he kept several secretaries busy bringing correspondence up to date and writing a history of the Volunteer Program of LDS Social Services, which includes his philosophy of volunteering.

One day I sincerely praised Charlie for his continuing Christlike involvement in the lives of others in the face of great pain and certain death. He smiled a wry smile and quietly said, "The Savior knew he was terminal, too."

When Charlie died, there may have been those who said that Charlie Stewart had given up the fight. Charlie Stewart never gave up on anything. He did not resign nor ask a truce; death did not come to surprise him or snatch him away. The Father took Charlie Stewart home when he had completed all that he was sent to do. Appropriately, he died on Thanksgiving morning.

At Charlie's funeral, Elder Robert L. Simpson quoted the following scripture:

> The spirit of the Lord God is upon me; because the Lord hath anointed me to preach good tidings unto the meek; he hath sent me to bind up the brokenhearted, to proclaim liberty to the captives, and the opening of the prison to them that are bound. (Isaiah 61:1.)

Those lines described what Charlie did with his short, beautiful life. No doubt they also speak of what he is still doing.

Charlie's body was laid to rest in the quiet peace of Meadow, Utah, the little town where he was born. I stood at the foot of his grave and there sang, for the second time that day, a certain song which Charlie had requested for the funeral services.

I looked out over the valley. The sun which was sinking in the west was at that very moment rising somewhere else. It was a fitting symbolism. My great and good friend had gone home to stand "on His right hand."

18   I Was in Prison and Ye Visited Me

Bart's story is a dramatic one. He was in prison. He was visited by missionaries of the Church. His life was completely transformed because they really cared.

"Brethren, if any of you do err from the truth, and one convert him; let him know, that he which converteth the sinner from the error of his way shall save a soul from death, and shall hide a multitude of sins." (James 5:19-20.)

Bart's story is transcribed from a taped fireside talk. He shares the dramatic story of his conversion to the gospel.

"I pray that what I have to say might stimulate our testimonies and give us a better understanding of the marvelous service that is done through the missionaries of the Church. I would like to give you a little background. Of course, what I have to talk about is my life — my life and how the gospel of Jesus Christ has affected it.

"I am one of eight children. The other seven grew to be good, honest citizens and parents. We had a wonderful mother and father, whom I caused seventeen years of suffering, heartache, shame, ridicule, and criticism because of my attitude and behavior. They continued to love just as my Father in heaven has continued to love, looking forward to the day when I would accept the truth and begin to live my life from that point. But because I wouldn't listen to their advice, to their constructive criticism, and because of my attitude and behavior as a youth, I have spent seventeen years confined behind prison bars for acts which I have committed against society, for being disobedient to the principles our Father in heaven has given us.

"When I was a teenager, I felt a great need to be accepted. Of course none of us likes to feel rejected, but I had a deep problem — an inability to communicate with people, even with my parents. I couldn't share with them my problems, my feelings of happiness or sadness.

"To gain acceptance of the group I committed outward acts of rebellion. I would ride down the street on a bicycle with a cigarette hanging from my lips, thinking that this made me a big man. I was one of the world's biggest fools. My rebellion took me from a state reformatory to the state prison, then to various prisons throughout the United States.

"Throughout my life in prison I still would not conform to rules; I still could not accept advice. I had become what was known as one of the 'hard rocks' in whatever prison system I was in. I was always taking part in riots, food strikes, and escape plots. I was continually in solitary confinement for my behavior.

"When I was returned to the prison for the third time, I was given an additional sentence plus a parole violation. I reached a point in my life where I had a sense of a great loss. I didn't understand that that loss was a deprivation of the right to make my own choices, my own decisions, to exercise the God-given right of free agency. In prison you are told when to get up, when to go to bed, what to eat, how much to eat, and how fast to eat. You are even told, in some prison institutions, how to smile. I recall one time I was given twenty-eight days in solitary confinement because I said 'Yes, sir' with a smile on my face. I was told my looks were insolent.

"As I sensed this loss, I became emotionally upset. I felt that I was breaking under the strains and tensions of prison life. I sought to seek release through escape. I escaped from the prison in 1957. Actually, I didn't escape from anything. I became a fugitive from justice. A fugitive lives under a greater tension than does a person confined. He is looking over his shoulder all the time. He lies to anyone he comes in contact with. He usually rides in freight trains, sleeps under bridges, eats out of tin cans. He lives with the constant fear of being apprehended and confined to prison again.

"I was apprehended and given ten years for my escape. Put on a chain gang to work on highways, I subsisted on a diet of grits and gravy, black-eyed peas, and corn bread. I lived in a cell block with filth and body stench. The guards were promised a lifetime salary if they took the life of an inmate during an attack or escape. Many times a guard would point a .30-30 at your belly and spit tobacco juice down your front or curse you and your family, then ask you if you wanted to do anything about it, hoping that you might make some attempt to either attack him or escape so that he could earn this lifetime salary.

"In June 1958 I decided to give a guard the opportunity of earning that lifetime salary. I had reached the point that not only was I trying to escape but I no longer wanted to live. Life had no value, no meaning. I had lost all hope. I knew that when I ran across a highway, the presence of a guard, armed with a .30-30 and a .38, would give me hope that my life would be taken and that I would be released from all my inner torments. But somehow, when I made the attempt, I overpowered the guard and relieved him of his guns. Once again I was a fugitive from justice, living the life of the hunted.

"This time on being apprehended I was transferred to a prison unit for incorrigibles. When an inmate has reached a point where he no longer stands a chance to be rehabilitated, no longer stands a chance to be an asset to society, to anyone or to anything, he is put in these prison units to protect society.

"In the winter of 1962 there was a riot and the prison was almost demolished. Because of the past pattern of my life, it was determined that my influence among the inmates had brought about this riot. I was given thirty days in solitary confinement. There my weight went from 160 pounds down to 132. When I was freed I came before the warden. He said, 'Robertson, as long

as you are in this state you will be confined to this prison unit.'
According to state law, the parole procedures made anyone
ineligible to apply for parole while confined in a maximum
security unit. I was told that I would serve thirty-seven years in
that unit.

"The unit was surrounded by double fences and guard
towers. Dogs patrolled between the fences, and every guard had
a dog trained in man-attack on leash. I have seen as high as
three hundred stitches required to suture a wound that some of
these animals have inflicted upon inmates.

"Inmates who work on a prison cotton and peanut farm live
under terrible conditions. The diet is malnutritious. They pick
cotton for ten hours a day. When they come in, they're actually
stripped of all their human manhood. They walk naked from
the change room to the cell block, where there is another
change of clothes, and they leave in the same way each day. The
tension and strain are so great that strong men break. Men cut
their own heel tendons to become crippled for life. I've seen
fingers and toes deliberately amputated by a sharpened hoe so
that men could be transferred to a prison hospital for a while,
where the treatment, and the food were just a little bit better,
where they could rest. They hoped that their self-inflicted
injuries would require them to be transferred to a different unit
where they would no longer be forced to pick cotton.

"After I was released from solitary confinement, there were
a number of letters for me. One letter was from my oldest
brother. He reaffirmed the love and concern of my mother, my
father, and my brothers and sisters. After all I had done, he said,
'We continue to pray that someday, somehow, you will be able
to accept our love and begin to rebuild your life.' He told me the
news about people I knew; and at the conclusion of his letter, he
asked me the oddest question I have ever been asked. He said,
'Bart, would you like to have the elders visit you?' I kind of
sneered inwardly and thought: 'What have the elders got to
offer me? Can they change these conditions in any way? Can
they take these emotional terrors, these strains and torments
from me?'

"In my return letter I did not acknowledge my brother's request; I made no mention of it. But I know that our Father in heaven answers prayer. Through inspiration, my family drafted a letter requesting that missionaries visit me and directed the letter to the General Authorities of the Church, who in turn sent it to the president of the mission in that area.

"The prison unit's security measures are so stringent that, regardless of how many miles your family has to travel, you don't know they are there until you approach them in the visiting room. If they make mention of it in their letters, it is censored. On a Thursday morning I was told to remain in from work. I was apprehensive, for inmates are requested to remain in from work only for a serious illness or an infraction of prison regulations. I felt certain that they had discovered something I had done wrong and that I was going to solitary confinement. I gave what little personal possessions I had to a friend and told him to keep them until my release.

"At about eleven o'clock that morning, two guards and their dogs came to the cell block. 'All right, Robertson', they said, 'you're wanted in the warden's office.' In my belligerent way, I shuffled by them and walked downstairs to the long lower hallway. Double bars separated the administration offices from the main body of the institution. As I reached the bottom of the stairs I looked up the hallway and saw four people standing there. Never in my life had I experienced the feeling that I did then. The Spirit of the Lord testified to me that these were LDS missionaries bringing me an opportunity for life.

"I walked into the warden's office, and as he was about to make introductions I said: 'I know who they are. They're missionaries from The Church of Jesus Christ of Latter-day Saints.' This took the warden by surprise, because he knew how tight his security measures were and he couldn't understand how I knew who the visitors were.

"The missionaries introduced themselves as Brother and Sister Adamson and Elders Jones and West. We talked about their drive to the prison and the welfare of my family. Then

Brother and Sister Adamson interrupted and said, 'Bart, what do you want in life, what are you looking for?' In my crude way, the only way I could communicate, I put up my thumb and said, 'I want them prison gates opened.'

"Sister Adamson smiled. 'That's wonderful,' she said. 'Is there anything else?' (As if that were just a little obstacle to overcome!)

"I was taken back and replied, 'Well, I would like to find peace and happiness.'

"The missionaries then told me: 'What we have to offer you this morning can give you peace and happiness. If you will accept Christ as your Savior and accept the gospel as the way of life, you can overcome any obstacles in front of you or any obstacle that will ever be in front of you.'

" 'You don't understand,' I said. 'I have nearly a lifetime to serve. The law states that I am not eligible for parole.' I continued on, pointing out the many obstacles. But the missionaries were not concerned about such things. 'We don't understand all of these laws and rules and policies', they said, 'but we do understand the promptings of our Father in heaven. As he is our witness, we promise you now that if you will accept his gospel, you will realize the opening of those prison gates and peace and happiness a lot sooner than you expect.'

"Actually, I sensed freedom long before the prison gates were opened, for my inner turmoils began to be stilled. I began to have hope for better things. The missionaries visited me several times. During one visit Sister Adamson sensed that something was not right and asked, 'Bart, are you praying?'

"I said, 'No.'

" 'Why not?'

" 'Well, I live in a cell block with forty other men.'

" 'Are you ashamed to pray?' she continued.

"Because of my inability to communicate, all I could do was shrug my shoulders. I tried to begin the conversation again with Brother Adamson, but Sister Adamson would not let it continue until she had made her point. She said: 'When you go to your cell tonight, will you kneel beside your bed and pray to your Father in heaven?' For the first time in my life I had come in contact with a person to whom I couldn't lie. I looked at her and said, 'Well — yes, I will.'

"At the time I thought I was pacifying a whim of Sister Adamson's. But that night I tossed and turned for about an hour and a half in my bed, wondering why I couldn't go to sleep. Then the events of the day flashed before me, and I recalled the visit and heard myself say, 'Yes, I'll pray.' I looked around the cell block, and as inconspicuously as possible, and for the first time in my life, I got on my knees and prayed. I shared with my Father in heaven my anxieties and my desires. I prayed for his help, his strength, his courage, and his wisdom. My parents had waited years and years for an answer to their prayers; I had to wait but a few moments. That night I slept restfully for the first time in years.

"I sensed an answer to my prayers in regard to my relationship with my fellow inmates and with the guards, but most of all with the missionaries. As they were teaching me the missionary lessons, I began to understand gospel principles; they began to have meaning. I began to realize the value of life, its purpose. I began to look forward to the future, knowing that there was a life better than the one I knew, a life in which I could find a reunion with our Father in heaven if I would live according to gospel principles.

"About two months later Sister Adamson said, 'Why don't you write a letter to the parole board?' I told her that the law and parole procedures didn't qualify me for a parole hearing, let alone a parole. She said: 'I don't know about that, but I would like to share with you an experience of this past evening. In the midst of our evening prayer Brother Adamson and I stopped and looked at each other and said that you should write a letter and ask for a parole.'

"I wrote the letter and to my surprise a few weeks later I was taken to another prison unit for a parole hearing, an act totally opposed to all the state laws and parole procedures. Two months later I was paroled back to the state of Utah.

"The policy in Utah is that a person must serve a minimum of two years of their escape sentence after they are returned before they are eligible for a parole hearing, provided they have satisfied their previous sentences. Nevertheless, in less than two years I was paroled from the state of Utah and I had not even begun serving time for my escape sentence.

"Even then the miracles were not over. I was wanted for a crime in Colorado. I had written a number of letters to the district attorney, pleading with him to dismiss the charge. He wrote and told me in no uncertain terms that upon conclusion of any sentence or sentences that I was serving I would be taken into custody for the purpose of prosecution because of the nature of the crime. Brother and Sister Adamson also wrote a letter to this district attorney. To them he replied: 'Dear Mr. and Mrs. Adamson: According to our files, there is no record of a crime being committed or a warrant being issued against the person you named.' Think of it! Even records were lost or destroyed when I complied with the Lord's gospel in attitude and behavior.

"Prior to my release from the Utah State Prison I wrote an evaluation of my life. At the conclusion I wrote the prayers of my heart: 'Continue to have faith in the Lord Jesus Christ. Be reunited with my family and loved ones. Find a job and desire to work. Find a good woman to be my wife and possibly have a celestial marriage.' All of these prayers have since been answered.

"I do have faith in the Lord Jesus Christ. I have been reunited with my family and loved ones; our relationship is full of happiness and love. For the first time in my life I can put my arms around my mother. I can kiss her and tell her: 'Mother, I love you. I'm so proud to be the son of such a wonderful woman.' I can put my arms around my father's shoulder and tell him, 'Dad, I have a problem,' then talk to him hours upon end. I have a job. It's a hard job, but for the first time in my life I find great happiness and great self-satisfaction in working and enjoying the fruits of my own labors. I have been blessed with a wonderful woman to be my wife. I thank my Father in heaven for her. I thank her for her love, her understanding, and her patience with me. We are working and praying for the day when we can go through the temple.

"I am grateful to four wonderful missionaries who visited me and freed me from prison, both spiritually and temporally. I am grateful for the Lord's compassion and love for the sinner. I am grateful for the miracles he has wrought in my life, especially for the miracle of the gospel that can change our attitudes and behavior, give us strength and understanding, and endow us with that gift without which life is sunk in darkness and gloom. That gift, which came to me through the great gift of love, is hope."

19 I Never Asked God Why

Maria was born in Brazil. Tragedy struck several times while she was still in her teens.

The words of Emily Dickinson may be applicable to her:

My life closed twice before its close —
It yet remains to see
If Immortality unveil
A third event to me

So huge, so hopeless to conceive
As these that twice befell.
Parting is all we know of heaven,
And all we need of hell.

— Emily Dickinson

Maria became acquainted with grief, but despair remained a stranger. Because her father taught her when she was very young to volunteer to help others, she was able to pick up the pieces when, with regularity, her dreams were shattered. Serving proved to be her strength through sorrows and trials. She held fast to her dreams because she believed that good deeds are always rewarded.

Maria Flores was born in Brazil. She tells her story in a charming, straightforward way.

"I was born ten years after my parents were married. Since I was an only child, every effort was made to make me happy. I had a beautiful home and everything else a child could ask for. I grew up with two cousins who were older than I. My aunt, a widow, was going to school, so she and her two children lived with us. I had a very happy family life. There was a lot of love, a lot of friends, and a lot of happiness.

"My father was very concerned about my education. He felt it was one of the most important things in my life. At the age of four I could read and write. At five I was painting in oils.

"My father was very influential in my life and in the lives of his family. People would frequently come to him for advice, for celebrations, or just for a visit. He taught me that there were some things I needed to do without pay; my daily work had to be done so that I could take care of my physical body, but I also needed food for my soul. This food came in the form of volunteer work — service to others. I began my volunteer work in Brazil in that country's volunteer program. My motto became 'To serve, help, love, understand, and smile.'

"At the age of sixteen I had finished high school and was preparing to enter medical school. I dreamed of becoming a neurosurgeon. Little did I know that the people and the diseases I hoped to help someday would become a real part of my own personal life, but not in the way I had hoped.

"One morning I awoke feeling quite sick. My back hurt and my right leg was very heavy, but this didn't stop me from going about my daily work. The pain didn't stop, however, and within a few days my legs and my left arm were paralyzed. I was told I had polio. Because of my interest in neurosurgery, I knew that only through a miracle could the polio be cured so that I could walk again.

"In the hospital I still managed to keep smiling, to look pretty, and even to try reading. My main concern was not to let my little cousins feel sorry for me. Although I was in a great deal of pain, I wasn't going to feel sorry for myself or let anyone else feel sorry for me.

"This painful disease had struck at a very active and exciting time in my life. I played basketball, swam, and loved to dance. I felt sad that I would miss these things but realized that it wasn't the end of the world.

"Upon my returning home from the hospital, paralyzed and in a wheelchair, my father called me down to his office that very day. I had always looked upon my father's office as his disciplinarian ground, so I was scared.

"But my father was a wise man. He was an architect and used his interest in this field to help stimulate my interest in life once more. He told me that before my polio attack my life had been like a beautiful livingroom. The room had beautiful white curtains, a piano, flowers in a vase, paintings on the wall, and was filled with music and children's laughter. Then one stormy day the wind blew through the window, destroying some of the furnishings. The piano was out of tune now, the paintings hung crooked on the wall, the vase of flowers was on the floor — but the room was still there. He told me that what I needed to do now was to pick up the pieces I had left and make a new life with them. Only I could help myself do this. I had to be strong and have great faith in my Heavenly Father.

"The advice about picking up the pieces had to be incorporated into my life a second time when my father died. This was a very difficult time for me because my mother and I had to leave our beautiful home and move to the capital city. I worked in the hospital, helping people who were paralyzed learn how to do everyday tasks for themselves. My instruction was a new experience for these patients in the hospital because they had formerly been taught by someone who was not paralyzed. These patients had found it difficult to identify with and trust their previous instructor, so it was a wonderful experience for me and the patients to work together.

"One day a man with whom I was working pinched me on the leg. I screamed from the pain. This caused the man to believe that I was not really paralyzed. He thought that I looked too healthy to be in a wheelchair. I had to set about winning the people's trust in order to help them help themselves.

"My greatest challenge in this hospital was to help a ballerina who had been shot by her fiance. One bullet had left her
paralyzed; a second bullet had killed her mother. The girl had
been unconscious for a few months before she finally came out
of the coma. I tried to work with her, but she was too materialis-
tic and didn't really care. I have always felt that you must want
to help yourself before others can help you.

"One day I was having a discussion with a blind lady and
this ballerina. We were discussing God, and they commented
on how cruel he had been to all of them. They asked me if I had
ever asked God why I couldn't walk. I told them that I had not—
I only asked God to show me things I could do. I never asked
'Why?' They called me a fool, and I went away feeling very
hurt.

"When I returned home that night, my mother told me that
two missionaries from The Church of Jesus Christ of Latter-day
Saints had been to the house that day and that they would
return with a very important message. I had read a lot about the
United States and especially about the pioneers. I had often
dreamed of being a pioneer myself. My favorite places, places I
longed someday to see were Utah, Mississippi, and California.
When the missionaries returned, I learned about Joseph Smith
and about the Mormon pioneers. I knew that the message they
brought was true. I was baptized a week later and soon became
the Junior Sunday School coordinator.

"At this time I was engaged to be married, but when I joined
the Church my fiance didn't have the same faith as I. He didn't
believe at all. This was another burden that was very hard to
bear.

"Before I joined the Church, however, I had won first prize
in an art show. The prize was a ticket to any European country
or any state in the United States. I had never used the ticket, but
after joining the Church I dreamed of going to Utah. I returned
my engagement ring to my fiance and set about making plans to
go to Utah. Arrangements were made for me to receive needed
treatment at the LDS Hospital in Salt Lake City. I only planned

to stay in Utah for three months, but after my arrival I found that the people were so wonderful that I wanted to live there always.

"After getting out of the hospital, I went to the LDS Business College. My tuition was paid for by many LDS families. I graduated with an associate degree in marketing and business management and went on to study at the University of Utah. I felt my straight-A grades to be a way of paying my debt of gratitude to the people who helped pay my tuition.

"While attending LDS Business College, once again I had an overwhelming desire to serve others. I felt that I could serve the foreign students who were going to school in Utah, so I started a club called the International Club, the goal being to serve others and make people comfortable who were away from their home and native land.

"I made many friends in Utah. One of them, a young man, was very special to me. But he was soon called to serve in Vietnam. After he left, I felt the urge to work with those who were close to Vietnam, so I volunteered to work for the Red Cross at the Veterans Hospital. Before long, the patients were calling me 'Sunshine' because I tried to bring a little sunshine into their lives. My young man never returned from Vietnam, but I continued the work that seemed to bring him close to me.

"One of my experiences in the hospital was with a young man who had lost his leg in a car accident. He had been a frogman in Vietnam, and had been an excellent skier. After losing his leg, he felt that his life was over. He didn't want any help, and he didn't want to help others. I told him that he could have a normal life again, that he could swim and ski once more. He didn't believe me, and I left him that day feeling that I may have promised him something which was not possible. I returned home and started calling friends and doctors, trying to find someone in the same position as this young man who had made something of his life. I was able to locate a man who scuba-dived with only one leg and a lady who skied with only one leg. I returned to the young man the next day and gave him the phone numbers of these people whom he could call and talk with about putting his life in order once again. I then turned to leave. The young man asked me to come back again; he said that he liked me. I told him that I would return when he started liking himself.

"Not all experiences can be happy ones, however. One evening a doctor at the Primary Children's Hospital called and asked me to come and translate for him. A mother who could speak only Portuguese was in the hospital with her nine-year-old son, who had a very uncommon disease. I was to tell the mother that her son was going to die, that there was no known cure for his brain tumor.

"When I entered the room, the mother just beamed at me and told me that she could tell I had good news for her. Knowing what I had to tell her, I found myself in an uncomfortable position. I took a deep breath, said a little prayer, and proceeded to tell the mother that her son would not live much longer. I also told her that when I first contracted polio the doctor had told my mother that I wouldn't live for another week; yet here I was many years later. I stayed for a while with the mother and son, talking and playing. Then I went home, tired and weary from the news I had been burdened with that night. To me this was my worst experience — to kill that mother's hopes and dreams by telling her that her son would not live.

"I have been able to do other things to help people besides my work at the Veterans Hospital. In the summer I collect clothes, toys, and old furniture. Some of my friends and I repair, repaint, and mend these items and give them to the needy. People who are sometimes afraid to ask for help from others often express their needs to me. I am more than happy to help these people if I can. I have even sent packages to Mexico and Honduras.

"I have made myself very independent and can do anything I want to do for myself. The reason why I won't let anyone wait on me is that someone can't always be there, so I must learn to take care of myself. I try not to have any 'can'ts' in my life. I feel that I constantly need to improve myself. My dream now is to complete the education which my father always stressed as being so important, to marry, and to have a family. I have faith that I will someday see my dreams come true."

Maria's dream did indeed come true. She married a worthy young man, also a convert to the Church. The youth in a Salt Lake City ward, with the help of the service and activities committee, gave her a beautiful wedding reception. A dear sister from another stake contributed two hundred dollars to help defray expenses. Many gave time, talents, and money. Her lovely wedding gown was a gift from a dress salesman. Maria remodeled it to fit. The bridesmaids furnished their own dresses.

That evening the cultural hall was transformed into a fairy-land of white and shocking pink. The flowers were arranged by a talented young adult. The refreshments were made and served by the youth. A beautifully decorated wedding cake was a gift. A Regional Representative of the Twelve played the organ during the evening. And 350 people came bearing gifts of love, admiration, and appreciation to the radiant bride who believes that, when you help others' dreams come true, yours will too.

20 The Debt of Wasted Yesteryears

Through surprising circumstances Tim found a small con-gregation of Saints called a ward.

They fellowshipped him in a wonderful way. They gave him love unconditionally and without judgment, and Tim dis-covered his true self.

"After I had been in the service the second time, I joined the mass of disillusioned young men and women who wander around rejecting the establishment and making a mockery of the ideals and dreams that make America great. I became in-volved with narcotics, prostitution, and organized crime. When I do something, I seem to think I have to give it all I've got, be it good or bad. I became a dealer in these vices.

"One day, without explanation and without any identifi-able motivating force, I left California and headed for Utah. It would appear that everything was waiting for me — 'set up,' so to speak. I was informed that I had come at a bad time of year for employment and that there were no jobs available; yet I got a job right away. I also found a place to stay rent free. At that time I wore long hair, a beard, and the mod clothing that was standard attire for the kind of people with whom I associated.

"Soon after my arrival, I went to the LDS Visitors Center on Temple Square. I don't know whether I was particularly inter-ested in becoming a Latter-day Saint, but a day or two after my visit I called the center and told them that I wanted to talk to somebody about the Church. They sent the stake missionaries. I was given the lessons; I became converted to the gospel of Jesus Christ and was baptized.

"The seventies in the ward where I lived were very interested in me and my conversion. During the time the stake missionaries were teaching me, they reported to the seventies about my progress. I was fellowshipped into the Church in a wonderful way. I had come to believe that the only people who really cared or knew how to show concern were those in the drug scene. To keep a brother 'on a trip' was their way of providing what passed for love. Fogged out on drugs, you think you belong to a close, warm 'world'; that is, until you want to get out. Then it can be terrible and extremely dangerous.

"But in my small community of Saints, my ward, was a group of people who were 'straight,' who loved me, who were really interested in me — the real me. They didn't ask what I had been, what I had to give them, or what they could get out of me. They loved me for what I was and what I could become.

"I was invited into people's homes for dinner, for family home evening, or just for friendship. I watched the parents and the children, comfortable and at ease with each other and with me. I was astounded to hear tiny children pray in words and meanings far beyond their years. I was really scared the first time I was asked to pray, but a little blue-eyed girl slipped her hand in mine and looked up at me. 'I'll help you,' she said. I participated in games I never knew existed — Monopoly, checkers, Old Maid, Rook, anagrams and dozens of others. I was part of the laughter, the teasing and the fun. I'd go home chuckling to myself and whistling aloud.

"I didn't know what was happening to me, but I liked the way I was feeling. I looked forward to family home evening. I never knew during the week where I'd spend the next Monday evening, but I knew I'd be invited somewhere. I can't explain what went on inside me as I observed and participated; I only know that new and beautiful resolves for my future family and myself were filed away to be used later. Most importantly, I learned my own worth. My self-esteem was elevated and it showed in everything I did at home, at work, and at Church. To be loved so sincerely caused me to carry the wonder of it in my heart, and it opened up my soul to the truths of the gospel. I came to understand the mission of the Lord Jesus Christ. I began to know myself as a son of God and desired to become like him.

"I became sensitive to the needs of others. None of us ever arrives at a place where we don't need encouragement and honest approval. I tried to give both to those about me, especially to the beautiful young lady who played the organ. A year after my baptism she became my wife. We were married in the temple. Nearly everyone in the ward who held a temple recommend came to show their love and support. We had to have the largest sealing room in the temple.

"I have become more actively and consciously engaged in living that brotherhood exemplified by the Lord Jesus Christ. I have come to know that all people have talents which can be used to help fill the needs of others. Regardless of who we are, we have something to contribute. The average individual undersells himself. I was hardly ever aware of my own ability to help other people until I began to reach out. I have discovered that the more I reach out and help others, the more I am able to reach inside me, the more I am able to identify myself and understand myself.

"Brigham Young taught:

> The greatest lesson you can learn is to learn yourselves. When we learn ourselves, we learn our neighbours. When we know precisely how to deal with ourselves, we know how to deal with our neighbours. You have come here to learn this. You cannot learn it immediately, neither can all the philosophy of the age teach it to you: you have to come here to get a practical experience and to learn yourselves. You will then begin to learn more perfectly the things of God. No being can thoroughly learn himself, without understanding more or less of the things of God . . . without learning himself: he must learn himself, or he never can learn God. (Brigham Young, *Journal of Discourses*, volume 8, pages 334-335.)

"Because I was loved I came to know the truth of that statement. Nobody ever knows much about himself until somebody loves him.

"I now feel an urgency to do something to contribute in the area where I caused so much destruction, both to myself and to countless others. I desire to do something to better the society in which we live. I believe almost everybody wants to do something to elevate social conditions, but they don't always know how. If everyone did one little thing, like pick up a single scrap of paper, pretty soon all the litter which detracts from our beautiful cities and rural areas would be cleaned up. But everyone has to help. In much the same way we can help lost souls such as I was. A little love here and an act of love there, everybody helping, and soon a life is made beautiful."

21 The Yellow Roses

O that we cared deeply enough to discern that there is a time when only a gift of "yellow roses" can help another pick up his burden and carry it another mile!

A newly widowed mother was visited by a couple who desired to furnish Christmas gifts for her and her three tiny children. She gratefully accepted their invitation and told them what the children wanted Santa to bring. She declined, at first, to acknowledge what she wanted, but after considerable urging she said that she wanted only one gift — a dozen yellow roses.

Privately, the wife of the giver said to her husband: "Nobody ever gives me yellow roses for Christmas. Who does she think she is, Lady Astor?" No one bothered to find out why the young widow wanted yellow roses.

The month preceding Christmas had been the most difficult since her husband's death. She had found the reality of his ever having lived slipping away from her. She kept thinking of the dozen yellow roses he had given her each Christmas. She desperately wanted to feel him close to her and thought that perhaps a dozen yellow roses would help his face come into focus.

For Christmas she received a nightgown and several pairs of hose. The givers never knew that she wept in desperation, not gratitude.

22 Father to My Brother, Mother to My Sister

One of the sweetest of our ennobling thoughts is that the heart of God our Heavenly Father is full of concern and compassion for his children. He speaks to us through the Holy Ghost and urges us to lift the burden of the suffering by becoming his instrument of compassion for all the lost, lonely ones who are his children, as we all are.

In a day when the success of marriage and the parenting of children are becoming secondary to the fulfillment of selfish, individual desires, more and more children cry out through deviate behavior for someone to take them into their hearts and homes and help heal their neglected bodies and wounded spirits with the nurture of God's love.

Dan and Brenda, young people untrained in the social sciences but trusting the Holy Ghost to teach them, have become father to their brothers and mother to their sisters.

I heard about Dan and Brenda before I met them. They take incorrigible teenagers into their home after others have given up on them. Their success in helping troubled youngsters change the direction of their lives is phenomenal.

One evening they came to visit me. Brenda was young and lovely, Dan was strong and self-confident. With them was their eighth child, a beautiful baby boy. Their love and respect for each other was apparent. I was surprised that they were so young. After I had visited with them, at my request Dan wrote the following heartwarming story.

"I was brought up in a humble home with six brothers and sisters. Our livelihood was made by milking cows and selling milk and cream. We usually milked about ten cows and made just enough money to buy sugar, flour, salt and pepper, and other basic commodities. Everything else we ate we raised or hunted. Jack rabbits we trapped and deer we would get during deer-hunting season were our main staples for the winter. It was a big job trying to support us. I stayed home from Church many times as a youngster because the soles of my shoes were worn out and we couldn't afford new ones.

"My father was the most generous man I have ever known. He displayed this generosity quietly and usually without reward.

"Because our farm was surrounded by the Ute Indian Reservation, the people who most generally needed help were Indians. Quite often we would pick up an Indian hitchhiking from town, and Dad would drive him to his home even though it might be twenty miles out of the way. Many nights we were awakened by some Indian knocking on our door, needing a ride to town or seeking protection for someone in his family who was drunk.

"Dad regularly cared for certain unemployed families and widows. He would hitch the horses to the wagon and load on potatoes, carrots, or whatever we had. He would gather from neighbors whatever else he felt was needed, then deliver it to those in need.

"Mother sacrificed so that Father could give. The greatness of a wife and mother can best be seen in the works of her husband and family. My mother never had many comforts; life was very hard for her. Every time Dad gave something away or spent money on someone else, she had that much less for herself and for their children, but Mother knew that our most important needs were spiritual and not material. She had tremendous faith. She truly supported the priesthood in our home.

"Having parents who were generous to less fortunate people is a wonderful blessing. Once in a family home evening class in Sunday School I heard the question asked: 'When neighbor children or relatives are playing with your children and take their toys away from them, should you, as a parent, teach your children to hold their own or should you let them be taken advantage of?' The consensus of the class was that a child should always be taught to take care of himself. I disagree. I believe that the greatest lesson a child can learn is that of giving and letting others have the advantage, if there is a choice. What a wonderful thing to be so generous that someone can take advantage of you!

"As far back as I can remember my father has had a chronic case of sugar diabetes. The blood circulation in his legs and feet was so bad that he couldn't get around very well, and they hurt him so much that he was very irritable most of the time. As a teenager I couldn't really understand his suffering and short temper. I ended up by running away from home when I was sixteen. I took up cigarettes and alcohol and became a regular law-breaker until I was sentenced to reform school.

"On the day I was sentenced, I was waiting in the courtroom to be taken to reform school when a friend of mine was brought in by two Marine Corps recruiters to obtain a release for him to join the marines. We chatted about each other's fate and I decided that if the judge would let me I would join too. The judge approved, and I joined the marines for four years.

"During my time in the marines, I met the special person who would later become my wife. Brenda was raised in an LDS home and was active in the Church. She had a very strong testimony. After I returned to my tour of duty, our relationship developed through letters. She did not know I had a Word of Wisdom problem.

"One evening Brenda called me from Washington and asked why I hadn't written and when we were getting married as I had promised. I realized that she might be my one chance to straighten out. I had her come to California. On the way to the bishop's house to get my recommend for a temple marriage, I told her my problem — that I wasn't worthy of a recommend. She cried a little, but we agreed to take the bishop's advice. I paid my tithing and attended Church regularly, but I continued to smoke for six months without Brenda knowing it. On the day I was discharged from the service I threw away my cigarettes, and I've never had another one. A year later Brenda and I were sealed in the Salt Lake Temple.

"Brenda and I have always planned to have a large family, and we set the number at twelve children. When I was twenty-seven, I became a volunteer for a youth ranch project. I interviewed boys at the county detention center who were candidates for the youth ranch. I wanted to help some of the boys and talked to Brenda about it. We decided that if we could have twelve children when we were older, it should be easier to handle twelve while we were young. Within a year and a half we had a dozen children in our home — six of our own and six 'borrowed' ones. We've had twelve or thirteen children continuously since then.

"I remember the day we picked up our first foster child. I had a meeting with the MIA teachers to plan a party and I told them I had to leave early to pick up a sixteen-year-old youngster from the detention center. For a half hour they all joined in telling me that we shouldn't take a sixteen-year-old boy because he would have a bad influence on our children. In rebuttal I asked the MIA teachers how many of them had been on a mission. Three of them had, so I asked, 'How young was your youngest convert?' That ended that conversation.

"Brenda and I believe that we all need help from others at some time, in some way, and that consciously or subconsciously we are constantly seeking that help. Remembering this helps us to be more effective. Even though we may desire to be perfect like our Heavenly Father, we just aren't strong enough alone. We are all weak in different ways, and it is by giving to others according to the talents given us that we find strength to overcome our own weaknesses.

"Sometimes we tend to feel that some people actually desire to do wrong, but I don't believe that is true. I think that they simply aren't strong enough to combat temptations in certain areas, or that they lack the maturity to compete with others or to face life's challenges. These are weaknesses, not rebellious desires. It is important to see the difference. When a person is rebellious and mean, Brenda and I try to see the tremendous potential that person has as a child of God and refrain from judging and ruling out the chance that, given love and proper opportunities, he can reach great potential. We have come to recognize that, even though we may not possess great confidence in ourselves, we may well possess the talents necessary to stimulate another's latent potential.

"Teenagers are vibrant, excited, and anxious to prove to the adult world and to their peers that they can excel in some area. They are usually successful. They excel at either good or bad, depending on their direction. Youth instinctively look to adults for guidance and direction, but they lack the maturity to compensate when they don't get it. The result is insecurity, which can cause kids to become dropouts. Seeking security through acceptance, they relate to those who have failed; in this way pressure on them is eased and their situation no longer presents a threat to their self-esteem.

"The question 'Why don't you act like an adult?' is commonly asked of the fifteen- and sixteen-year-old in the family, in school, or in Sunday School class. The main reason why he doesn't act like an adult is that he isn't an adult. Some of us spend most of our lives developing adult maturity. I never really became adult until I began to share and sacrifice. That thrust for me didn't occur until after I was married and our first baby arrived. Only then did I start living for someone else. So we mustn't expect twenty-one-year-old results from a sixteen-year-old. When I have successes with youth in our home and youth in Church programs, it is because I vividly remember my youth — how I felt about things and what my reactions were, how tough or tender my feelings were, and how many heartaches I suffered because I deliberately or unintentionally lost myself in a labyrinth of confusion heading nowhere.

"Many people are reluctant to take foster children because they may get close to them and suffer when they return them to their own homes. Foster parents need to love a child enough that it does hurt to see him go; but if that is the next step in the child's development they must want it to happen. It's a wonderful thing to help unite a mother and father and a seemingly lost son or daughter. You have to think often of how thankful you would be if your child left home and some good person cared for him and helped him develop an attitude of forgiveness and a desire to return home. You would be eternally grateful.

"Having had many foster children in our home has resulted in our developing certain attitudes we feel are essential for successfully changing the behavioral patterns of teenagers and bringing out their good traits. These can all be included in that great commandment, 'Love thy neighbor as thyself.' Isn't it a shame that we love our own little children so much but can scorn our neighbors' child and run him off and say that our responsibility is only to those born to us! All the children on the earth have a tremendous potential. Children are sent here to receive the blessings of earth life with adults as their guardians. Our responsibility is to everyone we meet, and our task is never completed until all of the sweet, precious children of our Heavenly Father have been brought back to him. Of course, we know that not all will return, but if we dedicate ourselves to helping our brothers the number that do return will increase.

"Attitudes and actions that have worked for us can best be illustrated by experiences with some of our foster children. Each one has a different need and each has taught us some great lesson and better prepared us for the next challenge.

"Our first foster child was a sixteen-year-old boy who, because of his home life, felt he had no identity — he was going downhill and no one really cared. He expressed this by dressing sloppily, teasing the little ones, and showing off continually. He would ask at midnight if he could go bowling or to play pool, and a refusal on our part meant days of sour attitude and arguing. I learned that going bowling or playing pool at midnight wasn't so bad. I went with him. We discussed things at those times which never would have been said under other circumstances.

"We learned to sit him in front of us, say 'I love you,' and then think of ways to demonstrate it. To do this we had to give up free time and privacy. That may seem a great price to pay for a spoiled kid, but this so-called spoiled kid is now a proud twenty-two-year-old husband and father. He has a two-year-old son whom they have taught to call us Grandpa and Grandma, and we're only ten years older than he is! He is making great strides in putting his life in proper order.

"Our foster children have taught us to rely on the Holy Ghost because they have caused us to face problems we've never studied about or experienced. One night Brenda and I decided to go to a movie for our weekly night out. We needed a baby-sitter and our twelve-year-old foster girl wanted to sit. She had asked before, but we didn't trust her. When we would have a sitter come in, she would resent it. On this evening I talked Brenda into letting our foster girl baby-sit because I felt that we had to demonstrate trust in her. As we left, Brenda proceeded to tell me all the reasons why she shouldn't be left with the responsibility and enumerated all the upsetting things the girl had provoked that day. As I listened, I too became upset. I turned the car around and drove home, prepared to tell the girl that she had to 'shape up.' Approaching the house, I thought, 'What is the right thing to do for her benefit and ours?' I listened for the still small voice to guide me. As we stopped in front of the house, I had a definite impression to go on to the movie and then call the girl on the phone and tell her what a fine person she was. This we did, and to our amazement when we called she had all the children sitting in a circle, playing games and having fun. We told her we loved her and appreciated her, and she was thrilled.

"Brenda and I learned that crises are great opportunities to reach foster children. Crises are their way of saying: 'You say you love me, but I don't believe it! Now prove it!' They have been creating these tests all their lives, and no one has loved them enough or been patient enough to prove they love them. When someone does, they start back up the road toward success.

"We've learned to accept foster kids as they are and to love them without their being perfect. Most of us say, 'I love you no matter what,' but too often we love them only when we can be proud of them or when they make us look good. Too many fathers want their boys to be great football players because the fathers love football; frequently their sons would rather be something else. We are so busy fulfilling our dreams and ambitions through our children that we forget that their desires and aptitudes differ from ours. Brenda and I have learned not to force kids to be Mormons or college graduates or anything else, but to tell them to be whatever they choose and to choose something that will bring them happiness. We then rely on our example as a family to give them the right desires. Our foster children who have been opposed at first to religion and the LDS Church have sooner or later attended church without coercion.

"You cannot take a person who is disillusioned with the adult world and with religion and put him under a strict set of rules such as: no smoking, attend Church, be in by 10 P.M. If you do, you either eat your words or end up sending the foster child back. Perfection comes slowly to those of us who have love and stability; it is much harder and slower for those who don't.

"Once when we were awaiting the arrival of a new foster child, the case worker informed us that the fourteen-year-old girl we were taking would stay out until four or five o'clock in the morning, and if she was restricted she would crawl out of the window. When she arrived we told her that we knew about her dating habits, that the policy of the Church was no dating until sixteen years of age, and that we agreed with that counsel of the prophets. We told her that we hoped someday she could comply with that policy, but until she could we didn't want her to climb out of the window or lie to us about where she was going. If it was important to her to go out, we would rather she go with our approval than to lie or be dishonest with us. At first she took advantage and dated every night, but gradually our love and her conscience won. Soon she was calling our attention to the fact that she was in a few minutes earlier than we had asked or that she hadn't had a date for two weeks. She is now married and is the mother of a cute little girl.

"When a person asks foster children to do things they aren't capable of, he is forcing them to lie to please him. I have yet to have a teenager admit to me that he is using drugs if I ask him point-blank before establishing that I love him regardless of his weaknesses. We had one foster girl who was using drugs very heavily, and as a result it was nearly impossible to talk with her. If any word was spoken that implied disagreement or displeasure with her, she'd become hysterical. This is common with chronic drug abusers. We recognized this, and so as not to alienate her we remained silent about drugs or the Church. We complimented her when she merited it and told her how refreshing and neat she was.

"Finally, after about two months, we were communicating well; so I decided that at the right moment I would talk to her about her drug problem. She was very excited one night about the good time she had had and told me about it as I stopped in her room to say goodnight. I felt moved that this was the time. I said: 'You have been with us a long time now, and we have never forced you to be a Mormon and we never will. We have loved you and treated you as one of our own because we feel you are. I believe that the gospel is true, and because of the gospel we have invited you to be a member of our family. Without the gospel I wouldn't be the kind of person I am. I hope that someday you will believe in it because it is true and because it can bring you the happiness and love for others that it has brought to me and my family. But you are free to decide on your own.'

"I continued, 'I know you have a severe drug problem.' She looked shocked and said, 'I don't either.' I explained how I knew, that I didn't hold it against her, and that if she chose to continue we would still love her. I told her that I hoped she would let me talk with her from time to time and maybe help her in this matter so that she could be genuinely happy. I explained that she, like everyone else, wanted to be happy and someday have a lovely family. She was concerned about how I knew so much about her and realized that I had a feeling about things and could tell when she was out of tune. We talked until one o'clock in the morning.

"After that night she began to change her appearance. In a short time she went from frizzy hair and black, skimpy clothes to attractive hairdos and long, pretty dresses. She visited the bishop, paid tithing, received her patriarchal blessing, and accepted an assignment as a Primary teacher — all this after 1½ years of hard, grueling pressure for us and her, interspersed with moments of beautiful success.

"Another important lesson we've learned is that many foster children do excellently for a while and then slip back. We pick them up and go again. Each time we pick them up they slip a little less and go a little higher before they slip back. It sounds like each of us, doesn't it? Our whole life is a process of climbing and slipping, and each time we hope to improve our average. These kids really live with the same needs as you and I, but they haven't found the help we have.

"When Brenda and I consider foster kids, we try to remember that they were told 'I love you' by a mom and dad who failed to prove it when they were tested. Some Sunday School teachers say, 'I love each and every one of you, and I will do everything I can to help you' — only to fail when given the test. Christ has said he loves us, and the gospel teaches that love is essential. But as emissaries of Christ and the gospel, many of us fail the test. How, then, can youth have faith in adults? Brenda and I feel that we adults have the task of demonstrating and proving that Christ, the Church, and adults can be trusted. Sometimes kids grow without help, but in those instances they usually carry so many scars and weaknesses that they can't withstand the pressure of striving for excellence.

"When I was sixteen and drinking and smoking and staying out late, I used to come home with my conscience so laden with guilt that it was almost impossible to enter the house. I would stand outside the door and wish a hundred times that I hadn't gotten drunk or smoked the cigarettes, and with all that guilt on my mind I'd go in. As soon as I did, my father usually started yelling at me, telling me how useless I was, and I would immediately get mad at him and forget all the guilt and remorse and blame him for my disappointments. I didn't usually forgive easily.

"On the other hand, my mother was always concerned and tried to help me. One night I came in late; I had been drinking again. Mother rounded up some leftovers from supper and warmed them for me. As I was eating, she sat down beside me and asked me if I had had a good time. I said, 'No, not really.' She said, 'How much did you spend on cigarettes and beer tonight?' 'I don't know,' I answered. She then asked if it would have been enough to buy her a new pair of shoes. She showed me her only pair of shoes; her toes were sticking out of the end and the sides were run over. She expressed her love and sent me to bed. My guilt increased, and I vowed to stop letting her down.

"Brenda and I have found that the greatest direction for successfully raising our children and our foster children is found in section 121 of the Doctrine and Covenants, verses 41 through 46. There it talks of maintaining influence over people only by persuasion, kindness and love and by the guidance of the Holy Ghost. I am particularly impressed by the reference verse 42 makes to 'pure knowledge.' I have never heard this phrase discussed, but I think it is the key to many problems with children. We can in no way judge what a child's needs are unless we have a pure knowledge and are nonjudgmental of the factors which made him the way he is. With foster children this is important to remember. After all, we have lived with our own children all their lives and have largely made them what they are over many years, but with foster children it is different; we must discover all that is in them in a short period of time. This can only be accomplished through the Holy Ghost. Without his help, earned and asked for, we will be guessing and will make mistakes — sometimes very costly mistakes.

"Another important lesson from the passage I have referred to is the significance to children of the stability which comes from parental consistency. Children must be able to count on parents to be consistent. This can be accomplished effectively if the Spirit is our constant companion. Only then will we act and react properly and say and do the right things for the right reasons. Children thrive on consistency in the home.

"Foster children who haven't had an understanding of the gospel cannot be judged by gospel standards until they have been taught them and understand them. Youth who use drugs and alcohol and who are immoral are not dirty, rebellious, and no-good. They cannot be committed to righteous principles unless they understand them. Therefore, we must be able to see through the sin, not accepting it, but understanding and loving the person behind it. We must go after that hidden potential by showing the gospel of Jesus Christ in our lives and teaching it by precept at the appropriate times."

Dan and Brenda have taken many unwed mothers into their home. One was a twenty-two-year-old girl. After the birth of her baby, she felt unable to give it up for adoption. Dan and Brenda knew that this usually is not a wise decision, especially for the innocent child who deserves two parents and a life without the stigma of illegitimacy. After making it a matter of prayer, Dan and Brenda said to the mother, "If you have made this decision prayerfully, if you have considered the child's needs before your own, then you both have a home with us as long as you need it."

The social-service worker was angry at this invitation. One of the agency requirements for placing unwed mothers was that the mother stay in the foster home for only a week or ten days after the birth of the child. But Dan and Brenda feel that they cannot turn away a mother and a child, leaving them to struggle alone. They have faith that if the girl continues to go to church and to live close to the Lord, one day she will qualify for all the blessings the Lord offers his children, including the repentant ones.

It takes courage, patience, sacrifice, commitment, and extraordinary faith to be father to our brothers and mother to our sisters. Yet our Savior said, "Whosoever shall receive this child in my name receiveth me." (Luke 9:48.)

23 A Joy Beyond Measure

Let the word of Christ dwell in you richly in all wisdom; teaching and admonishing one another in psalms and hymns and spiritual songs, singing with grace in your hearts to the Lord. (Colossians 3:16.)

I heard the group called Light sing at a fireside at the Assembly Hall on Temple Square in Salt Lake City. I knew immediately that they were not just performing, they were giving. I was deeply touched by the simple song they sang — a song about need and love and fellowshipping.

After the closing prayer, I asked Michael McLean about the song and how the group had come together.

"Sometimes," Mike McLean said, "we don't recognize an opportunity because it goes around wearing overalls and looking like hard work."

One of Michael's most rewarding invitations to create and give came at a most inopportune time. Some missionary experiences led up to this.

"When I reviewed my 'checklist of sacrifices' prior to going on a mission for the Church, I remember that the thought of saying goodbye to my piano was almost as painful as the thought of saying goodbye to my girl.

"Music, composition, poetry — all the creative arts — had been such a large part of my life that the thought of leaving them all behind for two years left me somewhat somber and melancholy. But I had dreamed of being a missionary and believed that what then appeared to be the 'sting of sacrifice' would be compensated by the joy of spiritual service. I've learned that one never sacrifices when one serves the Lord. If we could give him all we possess, we would still be in his debt.

"I had been in South Africa only a few weeks when the mission leaders decided to launch the family home evening concept as a missionary tool. A group of singing elders would be formed to help break down barriers and open minds and hearts to the message of the gospel. Elders Paul Nicholls, Roger Hoffman, Bill Evans and I began what came to be called 'The Family Band.' Our calling was to create a show that would captivate audiences of all ages with the message of family unity and to introduce them to family home evening.

"For six months we used song, poetry, comedy, and theatre, including scripture and words of the prophets, to communicate spiritually with the people of South Africa. The rewards of this service were thrilling. We were able to do the Lord's work through an idiom we had loved for our entire lives.

"This work, of course, was not to detract from but to contribute to and open the way for the essence of missionary work — the one-to-one testimony-bearing process in which heart speaks to heart by the power of the Holy Ghost. The purpose of the Family Band was to dissolve the preconceived biases people had against the Church; biases that had cheated them of the opportunity to be touched by the glorious message of the restored gospel. The Family Band experiences were deeply spiritual, but with an emphasis different from that which the usual teaching experiences bring to missionaries.

"After the Family Band was discontinued, the four of us reflected on the experience. The results so outweighed the frustrations and disappointments that we decided to get together after our missions and reach out to people through music and song. If we were to be successful, we would have to achieve a degree of professionalism that would be respected by all. We desired our music to carry an underlying theme of positivity and meaning. Our aspiration was that the Spirit speak through our music.

"After we all arrived home, we gathered from Kentucky, New Jersey, and California to Salt Lake City and formed a business called Light Productions. With a symbolism that is obvious, we chose the name *Light* for the group.

"While going through the struggles of recruiting personnel, going to school, and trying to get enough financial backing to get our business started, we grew in commitment and dedication to our goal. We wanted to speak to this generation in a language it understood and to say something worth listening to. We wanted to use our God-given talents to lift and serve.

"It was during these first struggling months that I had one of those all-too-few experiences of writing a song through the Spirit. I received a request from Dr. Charles Metten of the BYU Drama Department to see him in his office. It was near the end of the semester, so my workload was demanding. I wasn't too anxious to see him. Time seemed to be too fleeting to get everything done to which I was committed. But I stopped in his office on a lunch break.

"He told me that at the forthcoming Regional Representative Seminar the First Council of the Seventy was launching a program called 'The New Move-In Activity.' The idea behind it was that strangers who move into a new neighborhood are in need of fellowshipping through friendship, along with help, service, and acceptance. If we Mormons, especially priesthood holders, could put the gospel into action with meaningful service, we would gain the blessing of service, the new 'move-ins' would gain the blessing of being served and loved, and a door would be opened through which nonmembers would become interested in the Church.

"Dr. Metten was in charge of a presentation that was to illustrate how the idea could work. He and his associates had created a dramatization which was beautiful, but he wanted a song which would capture the essence of the vignette.

"Dr. Metten had heard a song I had written while with the Family Band which he said had deeply moved him. It was one of those songs in which the Lord did more of the creating than I. He wanted the song for this presentation to move people similarly.

"I tried to explain how busy I was, how impossible it was to meet his super-short deadline, etc., but this was to no avail. Finally I said I'd make an effort to write a song, but I emphasized that only a 'musical revelation' could bring it to pass.

"As I left Dr. Metten's office for my afternoon classes, an idea hit me; and a small melodic phrase raced through my mind. The idea was hazy and the melody unclear. It had something to do with two men. One needed help and love but didn't know how to ask for it. The other man wanted to give and share but didn't know how to go about it. I could imagine the first man singing, 'I need a friend,' and the other answering, 'I need to give.' That was all that came to me.

"After classes I searched out a piano so that I could work on what I believed was inspiration. Unfortunately, the 'well of ideas' seemed dry. No melodies and no lyrics came to me. I did some praying and then started digging up some old melodies that I'd composed long ago, in hopes that one of them would be a catalyst for the song. Nothing. Fasting, praying, and working didn't seem to help. I wrote two or three songs but none of them seemed to speak to the heart.

"Now I got down to it in greater earnestness and sincerity as I sought some privacy and a well-tuned piano. I discarded a flood of trite ideas. Then I went to my knees in soul-searching prayer. In essence my prayer was: 'Father, truths about the nature and needs of man can be revealed by the Holy Ghost. Please open my mind and heart to those truths, that this song might communicate spiritually with those who need to learn from it. The honor is thine; I am but the instrument. Please, please use me!'

"As I sat at the piano after the prayer, I reconsidered a few more ideas. One in particular seemed worth pursuing. I began selecting and rejecting phrases. The needs of those two men came into focus — their feelings became crystal clear; all I had to do was choose the right words to describe what my heart was seeing.

"When the song was completed, I sang it to myself. Halfway through the first verse my eyes became teary and my soul burned — I knew it contained truths inspired by the Lord.

"The words follow:[1]

(Sung)
Nonmember: I need to be a man, but just how at times becomes unclear.
    The man that's in my mind is fully independent and austere.
    He never asks for help in any way. Never begs or bows or cries or prays.
    He's not that way.
    That man's lived in my mind for so many years, it's hard to start
    To change the image now;
    I'm afraid my head can't hear my heart.
    But my family has followed me to this frontier (they depend on me);
    I can't let on how much I'm filled with fear . . . I'm alone,
    I need a friend (but I can't say that)
    I need a friend (but I don't want to convey that)
    And I don't know what to do . . . I don't know what to do to see me through.

Member: I need to live my creed, but just how at times becomes unclear.
    So often I'm afraid that my actions seem so insincere.
    Every Sabbath morn I vow to give,
    But my vows are not exactly how I really live.
    But then what can I do? I go to church, I don't hurt anyone.
    Somehow that haunts me, though, 'cause in my heart I feel more must be done.
    But in the world today no one believes
    You can help without a motive up your sleeve.
    And I need to give . . . I need to give,
    But I don't know what to do, and I don't know how or who to give to.

Nonmember: I can't find my own way home. Another day like this I'll go berserk.
    Where could this address be? Whoever made this map sure was a jerk.

(Spoken)
Member: Can I help you? I've lived in this neighborhood all my life . . .

---

[1]Copyright 1974 by Michael McLean. Used with permission.

but then again that's no guarantee . . . whoever made this map
was a jerk. Can I help?

(Sung)
Nonmember: I need a friend —

Member: And I need to give —

Nonmember: I need a friend —

Member: And I need to give —

Nonmember: And I don't know what to do.

Member: I don't know how or who to give it to.

(Spoken)
Nonmember: Yes, I guess I could use some help . . . I think I live around
these three blocks.

Member: I'm going that way . . . let me walk with you there.

Nonmember: Thanks.

Member: Are you new in this neighborhood?

Nonmember: Just moved in.

Member: Got a family?

Nonmember: Yes, a boy, two, and a girl, four.

Member: Great, I've got two boys, three and five. You know, there are no
kids around this neighborhood, and my kids could sure use
some friends.

Nonmember: So could we.

Member: Well, why don't you let my family and your family get together
tonight. We'll let the kids tear up the place and we parents will
supervise . . . sound good?

Nonmember: Sounds great!

Member: Tremendous . . . My name is Roger.

Nonmember: Mine's Paul. (They shake hands.)

(Sung)
Nonmember: I found a friend —

Member: God gave me you —

Nonmember: I found a friend —

Member: God gave me you —

Unison: And we know just what to do. We know we'll make it through.
He gave me you.

"Our group Light performed the song for the Regional Representatives and the General Authorities. We are requested to perform it often. It has been made part of a filmstrip that is touching hearts all over the world.

"The Lord could have touched his children with the same message in many ways, but He loved me enough to let me be part of the process. I love him, and I am grateful for the talents he has lent me.

"In a career of musical composition I pray that I am worthy to 'tap that Source' of eternal truth and that the things I write may be pleasing to God and move my brothers and sisters to love one another and worship him. Paul's words express my desire: 'Let the word of Christ dwell in you richly in all wisdom; teaching and admonishing one another in psalms and hymns and spiritual songs, singing with grace in your hearts to the Lord.' (Colossians 3:16.)

"Life is a wonderful experience — the Lord is anxious for us to do fantastic things and find fantastic success in his service. And he responds marvelously when we 'hunger and thirst after righteousness.'

"Best of all, he can use the talents of all of us. Mine happens to be in the field of music; others are gifted as patient listeners, wise counselors, leaders of youth, gospel scholars, good cooks, and in scores of other ways.

"No one is without the power to help someone. Everyone has the capacity as well as the opportunity to serve others. I am grateful for the experience which teaches me too that the Lord is willing to inspire any one of us in that service."

24 Sometimes Love Is a Kick in the Pants

Andy, a recovering alcoholic, must forever remember that shame and torture are but one drink away. His blunt, straight-forward story, told in his own colorful style, bears witness that serving others who are caught in the same diabolical trap helps to secure his own daily heaven-haven of self-discipline.

"It took years, but at last I admitted that I was an alcoholic. That didn't mean I was ready to call it quits. My first thought was that of combat — 'fight it out yourself.' I tried. It didn't work. As I grew older my drinking pattern became more complicated. I was coming up with a lot of physical problems. I had the shakes, my nerves were gone, and my thoughts were wild, even to the point of hallucinations. I knew I was in deep trouble, and I knew how I had gotten there. I could not truthfully lay the blame on anyone's doorstep but my own. That admission, however, did not mean that I knew what to do about it.

"I went in and out of hospitals to dry out. I was also with Alcoholics Anonymous for a period of time, but each time I failed to gain self-control. It seemed to me that I was a doomed man, that I would have to accept myself as such. 'Well,' I said to myself, 'you've just got to swaller it; that's the way it's gonna go.' When I got so bad physically that I was unable to navigate, I'd show up in the hospital, stay straight for a day or two, then start drinking again. 'Well, I'm just gonna die this way,' I thought. And that's what I made up my mind to do. I had nothing more to lose — I had lost faith in myself. But I guess the Lord didn't give up on me.

"I went on the hospital program for the last time before I gave up to die. I didn't receive too good a reception — I'd been a loser too many times. The hospital personnel treated me as though I was being court-martialed. They weren't too sure they wanted a character like me, and I wasn't too helpful. I flatly told them that I didn't think I had much chance. They imposed a few restrictions on me.

"The hospital personnel took me to Doc Hatton's ward to dry out. The doctor told me, 'I'd better keep you a few extra days this time.' I was really on the ceiling. Finally, after about eight or nine days, he gave me a physical examination. I was a little bit batty and foggy. The doctor looked up with a pleasant smile and said, 'Andy, I can't find much physically wrong with you.'

"My heart sank! I was in a despondent mood. 'I was starting to hope maybe a guy could kill himself by drinkin',' I said. It was then that I realized I wasn't gonna go that easy; it was gonna be a long, hard, drug-out, dragged-out battle. I was devastated. I had seen death as the easy way out of my suffering and misery.

"Sometimes love's a kick in the pants. The Lord seemed to be trying to tell me something, and that jolt got the message through. I began to take a look at my life and my attitudes. I realized that I hated everybody, including myself. Yet a little part of me, which I kept trampling on, persistently wanted someone to really care about me. That need kept surfacing.

"Through periods of life I had come to visualize most people as quite mercenary and cruel. I had seen all the bad parts of human nature many, many times. Whether I had avoided or had not seen the good parts, I couldn't tell. I could tell, however, and in great detail, just how freaked-out human nature was, including my own.

"As I was getting over the worst stages of drying out, a Brother and Sister Benton came to visit me in the hospital. It was obvious that what they didn't know about alcoholism could fill a good-sized book. I started to act disgusted; but there was something different about them. I analyzed it and wondered, 'Now, just what are they here for?' I waited to see. I first expected them to lay it on me about drinking. They didn't. They kept coming to visit me, and I realized that they were there out of love and fellowship. That was the part that got me, for I had been claiming that love and fellowship were sorely lacking in human nature. Yet there it was, right before me.

"It wasn't any one particular thing they did which helped me; it was the spirit that I felt from them. It was the fellowship, their acceptance of me as though I was as good as anybody else, and the fact that they really cared; which is all part of love, as I see it. After my release from the hospital, they invited me and another fellow alcoholic to their home for dinner. We felt welcome. It was a new, warm feeling inside, the dawn of new beginnings for me.

"I stayed in close contact with this fine brother and sister. As I gained self-control, I gained self-respect. I began to work with other alcoholics. I wanted my alcoholic friends to realize that rehabilitation was possible for them too. I have attempted to follow in Brother and Sister Benton's spirit, not to copy their style of giving love and fellowship but to come up with a style of my own which I found to be fitting and helpful.

"Recovery centers are merely first-aid stations for treating battle casualties. Nearly everybody who is around an alcoholic is involved in the disease in some way. When you cure one drunk, you cure a dozen other guys. It would appear to me that we've got to give all the help that's available. Alcoholics shouldn't have to meet together to hit the bottom before help is available to them.

"I am now serving as resident manager of an alcoholic support home. It's rather like a finishing school. When alcoholics are referred to our center, they have, you might say, flunked graduation from some other recovering program. When they come to me, they generally have got their little action, whatever it may be, fairly well put together. A support

house is a minimal security center. I merely ride fence, keep the
pace, smooth the edges, and interfere very little in patients'
everyday lives. When I am called on for advice or anything else,
I give it, but I don't volunteer it. Privately, though, I conclude
that there may be some sweeping changes going on inside some
of the men.

"I find that I feel more helpful when I am, as you might say,
on the firing line — helping a guy, one-to-one. I put myself in a
position so that they, I hope, feel we are on the same level. By
that I mean that I don't preach down to them or come out with
profundities. I let them know I can talk their kind of language
because I, too, have been in their situation; and that I am there
for one reason — to give help if they want it. The knowledge
that sometimes I know I help some brother to rehabilitate his
life can't be compared with any other reward. It keeps a guy
'plugging' down the right road.

"A long time ago I was in the U.S. Postal Service but had to
resign because of my drinking. When I went to the postmaster
and discussed my rehabilitation with them, they granted me
reinstatement rights. I asked them to allow me to work on their
alcoholic problem. They said they didn't have one. I said,
'You'll probably insist you don't have any alcoholics, but I
know different; there are alcoholics everywhere.' They agreed,
so I'll be going in to 'throw' mail part of the time and help my
fellow alcoholics part of the time. Those guys, and women too,
for that matter, are not the full-blown, hard-core types I'm
familiar with. They are maybe just getting a good start and so
are easier to get to and help. It's like any disease: the sooner you
get to it and treat it, the less the damage and the better the
chances for recovery.

"Now, I know, particularly in the LDS faith, that those who
don't understand the gospel are quick to lay the indictment of
sin on a guy when he's a drunk. That's a poor time to be laying it
on. Inside he's already laid that indictment on himself, and he
doesn't need anybody else's help to do it. I guess one of the
things I'm trying to do is show that you don't have to be a
psychologist or a psychiatrist to help people. The big secret is

in fellowshipping and giving. To get a guy started on his way is not too hard if you really sincerely love him enough to care. You can give him reasons why everybody else thinks he ought to sober up, but you've got to help him come up with some reasons of his own; you have to lead him to discover that he wants to stay sober. From then on it's a matter of continuing love and fellowship.

"I try just to keep going and working where I'm needed by alcoholics. I jump into any problem I think I can help solve; then if it looks a bit too hot for me, I hunt somebody up who I think might know what to do.

"Then, of course, I've got kind of a curious belief. I go along with repentance. And it doesn't make good sense to pull some caper or other and get all shook up and repent, or call it repentance, when a month later you pull the same thing and re-repent. My own point of view is that an individual is responsible for his actions and will be held accountable. That doesn't mean that when he fails he should quit trying; it means he should take repentance seriously.

"Now for some food for thought for members of the Church or of society in general who feel a need to get involved in helping in the field of alcoholism. The basic principle, I would say, where an alcoholic is concerned, is getting more familiar with this vicious disease called alcoholism. Don't lighten it. In other words, when a person is in deep trouble with alcohol he's nuts too — he's crazy. Therefore, you are not dealing with a rational person, and you've got to realize that. Some of them are shifty and conniving, others hurt, and others are being swept along to disaster and death. There are ways of learning the basic psychology of an alcoholic. I would ask a person to pray, to be deeply committed to helping and then not worry too much about failure. Many times you're not going to reach success the first time, and that's no fault of yours if you've laid the principles out.

"Any approach to help the alcoholic that is devoid of something spiritual, in my opinion, is precarious and may not work. What this spiritual thing may be is different with each guy; but there has to be some spiritual readjustment, some spiritual commitment made by the individual. Help him to read the scriptures; teach him to pray by praying with him; get him involved in his church; and then, as he's ready, give him an opportunity to help others with their problems and temptation.

"A guy's praying, I guess, is his own private business. I indulge in it. Sometimes I don't think I get any answers, and other times I come up with answers that hadn't occurred to me before. I guess what I ask is for somebody to send me down a dictionary of what I'm supposed to do so I can be right all the time, but I don't think that will happen.

"There's an element of timing in helping people, and the helper should be ready to move at any time. But that doesn't mean action right now is always the solution. When a guy calls you at three o'clock in the morning from a hotel room (I've had calls from someone who was so drunk he could hardly get off the bed), it isn't going to hurt any if he stays put till morning. A person has got to recognize the need. The guy might be sober, though, but you can soon tell. You can tell somehow, in the tone of his voice, that he means what he says. But as far as getting help, a person's got to be ready for help before he'll take help.

"What the alcoholic needs, primarily, is to be put under medical surveillance. That's the first thing: find out all the places where medical treatment is available; keep a written list. Then, when you've got a person who should get to treatment, you can get him there as quickly as possible. Some may be in serious trouble, some may not. Most of them think they are in great trouble, naturally. But that's not for you to decide. For myself, I am acquainted with every place I can stash a guy in this whole area. After he gets unclouded he may not want anything to do with me, but I'll let him tell me that. I'll give him the opportunity to reject me, but I'll let him know I'm always available.

"When working with alcoholics, you certainly have to have an unquestionable love for the individual you're working with. It's easier to love some than it is others. We are commanded to love one another, but that doesn't mean we've got to like everybody. I class that the difference. You may deal with people that you don't particularly like too much, but that shouldn't stop your efficiency in any way; you may learn to like them; they may learn to like you — who knows? So, in brief, I'm for banging away at this thing with anything that will work.

"I don't feel we have a utopian answer for the problem of alcoholism — not at this point. From where I sit, it looks like a long, strung-out battle campaign. The only way you win campaigns is to fight them out — right down the line. Maybe you think you're losing sometimes, but that's nothing. You aren't losing as long as you're fighting. But once you get this drunk on his feet — referring principally to me — it's up to him, you see, to devise his own system or way of going; otherwise, it is all for naught. I'll take that back. There are alcoholics who will remain medically dependent for the rest of their lives, and they should be accorded the treatment they need. But generally speaking a guy has to get on his feet and figure out what he is going to do to stay there and then do it.

"Now that I've got sobriety, I want to give it away to those who want it. There were a lot of people involved in helping me over the years. Hundreds of people propped me up in various ways. I can only show my gratitude by giving to others. I've got not only a new way of life; I've got something to give.

"Everyone who gains sobriety, hopefully, is another member of the team to help others. That's what he owes, according to me. That's what I owe. There's no other way of paying the bill. But not only do we controlled alcoholics have the obligation to help our fellow alcoholics. So do people who are not alcoholics. We are taught to be our brother's keeper. It isn't easy. But if we don't care who gets the credit, there are always ways to help somebody down the road of life.

"And we all need help. Perhaps we all need to help, too — it could be a need born in us. I guess it's hard to analyze why we assist others. The important thing is that we do it, not why we do it."

25 Could I Do Less Than the Savior?

I have a friend whom I dearly love. Her life-style is far removed from the teachings of her childhood. Her face is old with lines of dissipation and bitterness. "Why," I asked her, "do you continue to suffer? You're bitter and unhappy. Have you never had the desire to repent?"

Her laugh was harsh and without humor. "Oh, yes," she said. "When I was eighteen years old, before my sins were very big and my conscience was still able to hurt, I really wanted to repent. I tried, but the people who should have cared about me most wouldn't allow it."

"Wouldn't allow it?" I asked incredulously.

"They wouldn't let me repent. They kept alive and growing every mistake I ever made. I guess it made them feel righteous and holy."

I wondered if ever I had not allowed someone to repent. Velda is an example of one who gave that divine gift, and in giving it she affirmed her faith in the atoning power of the Lord Jesus Christ.

"Let us not therefore judge one another any more: but judge this rather, that no man put a stumblingblock or an occasion to fall in his brother's way. (Romans 14:13.) .

"Don and I heard about each other before we actually met. When he was released from prison he rented an apartment in our neighbor's basement. The neighbor and my mother were good friends. Don didn't tell his landlady that he had been in prison. She told my mother about the nice, good-looking, friendly, kind and considerate young man who had moved into her basement. She made a special project of telling him about me — the girl next door who was a member of the Church, a good cook and homemaker. Neither Don nor I realized she was playing Cupid.

"One Sunday afternoon in June his landlady called and asked if we were going to church. My mother said, 'Of course.' The neighbor said, 'Well, maybe I'd better tell you, then. The nice young man living in my basement has not been out of prison for very long.'

"As I was getting ready for church I was thinking: 'Just got out of prison and he's going to church! He's going to speak in church.' It didn't make sense to me. I wasn't remembering that Heavenly Father loves all his children — even those who have made serious mistakes and have spent time in prison.

"When we arrived at the church, Don was sitting on the stand with another man. As sacrament meeting started, I could hardly wait for the speakers. Our bishop introduced Bishop Heber Geurts, who told us a little about the family home evening program at the prison and about the progress and change Don had made in his life. He also mentioned that Don had been going with a girl, and he anticipated that they would be married around August. Don then bore his testimony, and the Spirit convinced us of his sincerity and of his exciting, new knowledge that the gospel was the only way to happiness in life. As soon as Don finished, our bishop asked us to extend the hand of fellowship and welcome Don into the ward.

"I was under the impression that Don was as good as engaged, so I didn't take much interest in him. This made him think I was stuck up. Our love story could have ended right there; but, living next door to each other, we couldn't help running into each other. It was summertime — days to lie in the sun and read, or work in the garden. Don would stop and talk. We spent many hours learning about each other and getting acquainted. He told me all about his past. It was kind of funny, though, because he told me that his past seemed like a play acted out by a person entirely unrelated to him. He was so nice that I couldn't imagine him doing all the things he told me he had done. For some reason that surprised me at the time, I didn't turn away from him.

"Don became very active in the ward. He spoke in various sacrament meetings and firesides throughout the state, telling people about the family home evening program at the prison and bearing witness of the miracle of repentance.

"His ward assignment was Sunday School teacher for the twelve- and thirteen-year-olds. Anyone who has taught that age group knows what a challenge they can be. Don stuck with those kids for almost a year, and they all adored him. He spent hours worrying about them and the direction some of them were taking. He cared about what they were doing and how he could strengthen them. But the class members were concerned about keeping their reputation. They had had about six Sunday School teachers in six months, and they were making bets among themselves as to how long Don would last. Don accepted their challenge and for the first time in his life he stayed with a Church calling.

"Don also got involved with the elders. He played basketball with them and built a good relationship with the fellows his own age.

"A couple of months passed before Don asked me out. I was apprehensive; in the back of my mind I was entertaining the ex-con image that people generally have. I was even a little scared. My fears were soon allayed, however. Don has since teased me about my being a little disappointed when he didn't take me up the canyon and try to slit my throat or something. He didn't even take me up the canyon. We went to a fireside. That was a beautiful beginning to our dating relationship.

"In the next few months, we had good times together — long talks and happy evenings making popcorn and watching television with my family. It had been so long since Don had enjoyed a family atmosphere that I believe he enjoyed being in my home more than going out somewhere.

"I had many different thoughts about Don as we got acquainted — mostly positive ones. I thought what a nice person he was, and how kind and considerate he was to take my widowed mother with us when we went to places like the movies or on temple excursions. And I thought, 'Someone who's that considerate of somebody else's mother can't be all bad.'

"We fell in love, and in May of the next year we became engaged. On June 29 Don took me to the Salt Lake Temple where we were sealed for time and all eternity. I'm glad I didn't know Don four years earlier. I wouldn't have liked him then, let alone married him. The life he was living then, without the gospel, was so different from the life he's living now.

"I've had many people ask me how I felt about Don's background — if it ever bothered me or if I was ever worried or concerned about it. Other than one time, I honestly must say no. That one time was just before we were married. I began to wonder if I was doing the right thing. I went into a kind of panic. I have since learned that most brides have similar moments.

"About a week before we were married Don and I had a little argument. I was tense and concerned about being sure that I was doing the right thing. Suddenly, my eyes lit upon the marvelous book *The Miracle of Forgiveness* by President Spencer W. Kimball. I had received it as a gift the previous Christmas. I had glanced through it and had read passages here and there but had never really studied it. Now I read the whole thing in one night. The one fact that came through clearly to me was that, although Don had sinned, he had repented, and the Lord had forgiven him. Could I do less than the Savior?

"From that point on I have never been concerned about or felt that I had to apologize for Don's past. All I care about is what he is today and what I know he will be in the future. No one's past should make a difference in how we treat him today. When Don and I meet and become acquainted with new people, they cannot believe that he was ever in prison; they always think we're pulling their leg. I think this is an evidence of the great change in Don.

"I can see other changes in him. For example, he has told me that a few years ago he didn't care if he had a job. Now he figures that he's late if he isn't there half an hour early! I think that shows quite a change in attitude.

"At the time of writing, Don is elders quorum president. He has a beautiful testimony of the gospel. He has helped my testimony grow. Many times when I might have been tempted to stay home from sacrament meeting, he has reminded me that just once is how inactivity starts. He says that's how all his problems started — just one thing at a time. That's the way Satan works.

"Don has told me many times that he wasted ten years of his life by being inactive in the Church. He is really trying to make it up now and lives the gospel to the fullest. He gets excited about paying tithing and contributing financially, as well as giving his best effort to the Church.

"Not long ago Don and I ran the Colorado River through the Grand Canyon. Most of the people on the expedition were non-LDS. The nonmembers were quite intrigued by us Mormons. One fellow in particular seemed very interested in Don and me. He watched us, the way we did things together and for each other, and the kind and considerate way we talked to each other. Apparently he had never experienced this in his own marriage. Don later said to me, 'We will always have to be a good example because we never know who's watching.'

"Sometimes Don is delightfully surprised about the change in himself. I remember one evening when we took our MIA group rollerskating. Don was skating with fifty teenagers, and they were trying to trip and harass him. I reflected how heartwarming it is that kids will harass and tease someone they love. I remember looking over at Don; he was nearly in tears. He skated over to me and said: 'Those guys in the "joint" don't know what happiness is. If they could see me now, they wouldn't believe it.'

"One of the biggest things Don has learned is respect for himself and other people. 'It's amazing how high you can hold your head,' he says, 'when you're doing the right thing. You don't have to duck your eyes; you can look everyone squarely in the face. How free you feel, how well you sleep when you're living the gospel and doing the things the Lord would want you to do!'

"Don has also gained respect for other people. I remember that when we were first starting to date I would do little acts of kindness for him. He couldn't imagine what I wanted — what was in it for me. He finally realized that I did things for him because I liked to, and he began to do little thoughtful things to make me happy.

"Don has always been a gentleman. The only time he really raises his voice toward me is when I open my own car door or when I do heavy lifting that I should leave for him.

"For the first time in his life Don is saving money. I've never been very good at saving money either. It tickles him to watch our bank account grow. It's difficult to realize how important or how rewarding the good and beautiful things can be to one who has never experienced them before.

"Don and I are looking forward to being parents and knowing we'll have our children for time and all eternity. We look forward to raising them in the gospel and teaching them the love and respect for family that was lacking in Don's life. We spend many hours just talking about our future and about the love we have for each other and for the gospel. We're in love. We're adjusting to each other. We're happy. We're growing in the gospel of Jesus Christ. I will ever be grateful to those wonderful people who cared, who prayed, and who gave their love to one of 'his sheep' that was lost and 'now is found.' Don has found the Savior, the gospel, himself, and me.

"Each day, and with a joyous heart, I pledge to Don my eternal love."

26 My Grandmother's Song

At times I believe that my grandmother knows that the gift she gave as she was dying has had a profound influence on my life.

When I was seven years old, my grandma died. Her right side had become paralyzed years before I was born, but her mind was keen. The stroke had also affected her speech, but as a little child I could understand what she said. I loved her.

I knew Grandma was dying. The grown-ups were inside her bedroom — the door was closed. I stood in the hallway outside Grandma's room, a desolate, bewildered little girl, looking out of a glass-paned door at a wintry world.

Then I heard someone singing. It was Grandma. I can still hear her voice, strong and melodious, coming to me down through the years. It was as though she was giving me a gift — not to me exclusively, but inclusively, a gift meant for all her posterity and for the whole world.

HAVE I DONE ANY GOOD?

Have I done any good in the world today?
Have I helped anyone in need?
Have I cheered up the sad, and made someone feel glad?
If not, I have failed indeed.
Has anyone's burden been lighter today,
Because I was willing to share?
Have the sick and the weary been helped on their way?
When they needed my help was I there?

There are chances for work all around just now,
Opportunities right in our way.
Do not let them pass by, saying, "Sometime I'll try,"
But go and do something today.
'Tis noble of man to work and to give,
Love's labor has merit alone;
Only he who does something is worthy to live,
The world has no use for the drone.

Chorus

Then wake up, and do something more
Than dream of your mansion above;
Doing good is a pleasure, a joy beyond measure,
A blessing of duty and love.

(Will L. Thompson, *Hymns, The Church
of Jesus Christ of Latter-day Saints, no. 58.)*

27 To Give More Purely

King Benjamin admonished his people to keep the name of Christ written in their hearts. "For," he asked, "how knoweth a man the master whom he has not served, and who is a stranger to him, and is far from the thoughts and intents of his heart?" (Mosiah 5:13.)

One hot summer day Marc's father led Marc to discover a truth that helped him purify his motives for giving:

"Let your light so shine before men, that they may see your good works, and glorify your Father which is in heaven." (Matthew 5:16.)

That scripture gives the pure reason for giving – to glorify God.

In his novel, The Brothers Karamazov, Dostoevsky has one of his characters, a noblewoman, confide in Father Zossima that she has often dreamed of giving her life up to service as a nurse.

> "But could I endure such a life for long? I . . . ask myself . . . And if the patient whose wounds you are washing did not meet you with gratitude, but worried you with his whims, without valuing . . . your kindness, began abusing you and rudely commanding you, and complaining to the authorities about you — which often happens when people are in great suffering — what then? Would you persevere in your love or not? And do you know, I came with horror to the conclusion that, if anything could dissipate my love for humanity, it would be ingratitude. In short, I am a hired servant, I expect my payment at once — that is, praise, and the repayment of love with love. Otherwise I am incapable of loving anyone."

(Fyodor Dostoevsky, *The Brothers Karamazov*, Signet edition [New York: The New American Library, 1957], page 61.)

We can readily identify with this woman in her need to receive rewards for her good deeds. We feel justified in turning away from a person who doesn't appreciate us. The need to be praised is human. But that is not the higher way.

Paul spoke in plainness when he told us to whom honor for good works should be given:

> [God] make you perfect in every good work to do his will, working in you that which is wellpleasing in his sight, through Jesus Christ; to whom be glory for ever and ever. (Hebrews 13:21.)

The story of Marc helps us know if our giving is for the right reason.

"My father died in April. After the funeral my two brothers, my sister, and I talked about the legacy Father had left us. It was not a legacy of money — there was enough to take care of Mother, but nothing much beyond that. The true legacy was the man we knew him to be — gentle, strong, wise, and patient. The touching, teaching moments we had shared comforted us, but they also made us ache with sharp, brittle bursts of pain. We were already lonely for him.

"I fell silent, remembering a hot summer day when I was seventeen. We had been hauling hay from the pasture up by the lake. I turned off the tractor, and Dad and I sat in silence, wiping the perspiration from our necks and faces. It seemed as though there was no one in the whole world but the two of us and a lazy bee that kept buzzing around my left shoe which was all green and wet from clover and new-mown hay.

" 'You've been troubled the last while, Marc,' Dad said quietly. 'Want to talk about it?'

"I did and I didn't. I didn't because I knew that the mixture of frustration and anger I felt would spill all over the place, and I might even cry. To cry at seventeen was a weakness of such magnitude that it could ruin a kid's whole life! But I needed to talk about it because I wanted someone to tell me how great I was and how ungrateful Paul was. The need for praise won.

" 'You know how mixed up and stupid Paul's been this last year,' I said. Paul was the fourteen-year-old son of the widow who lived about a mile down the road. 'You also know how many hours I've put in to try to help his mother harvest their potatoes. I even delivered them to the market over in Center-field — got up at four o'clock in the morning so I could be back in time to do the milking before breakfast.

" 'I've gone out of my way to make friends with Paul. His mother has been worried almost out of her mind about him. I've spent hours with him. I've taken him fishing and got the kids to let him play ball with them. They didn't want him, but I talked them into it. I told Paul he'd better be dependable and not miss the practices.

" 'I thought after I'd stuck my neck out for him he would go along, but he didn't. He's been learning to smoke and drink. I gave him heck one time when I caught him puffing on a cigar, and he got sick all over the front of my shirt. Then just when I thought he was doing pretty good, he got in that fight over at the show house. I thought maybe he was acting up because he had to wear hand-me-down clothes and all that. One Saturday I took my week's pay and went to town and bought him blue jeans and that red shirt I have been wanting. He didn't even thank me — not for the clothes or for the hours and hours I've spent with him trying to be friends to him, trying to show him where he's wrong. You'd think he'd show just a little gratefulness for all I've done.'

"I tried to act like it was sweat running down my face, but Dad knew it was tears.

" 'Hurts, doesn't it,' Dad said, 'when somebody doesn't say thanks for all you do for them.'

" 'Sure does,' I said, bawling right out loud. 'I'm never gonna help anybody ever again in my whole life. I mean it, too.'

"Dad let me cry a while; then he said, 'Marc, what made you want to help Paul in the first place?'

" 'Cause he needed it! And so did his mother. Paul's really a good kid, just plain dumb sometimes.'

" 'What made you think you could help?' Dad asked.

" 'Well, Paul's always kinda looked up to me, and I found myself thinking about him a lot and the way he was messing up his life. He's gonna get into real trouble, Dad, if he keeps on going the way he is.'

"Dad said, 'Do you want people to think you are great, or do you sincerely want to help Paul?'

"I was angry. 'Course I want to help Paul.' That was true, but there was also truth in Dad's other statement. I did want people to notice and comment about how great I was.

" 'Do you think a person should be worthy of his hire?' Dad asked.

" 'What do you mean?' I said defensively.

" 'Do you think people should seek pay for everything they do?' Dad asked.

" 'Well, I didn't ask to be paid for helping Paul's mother or doing his work. I certainly didn't ask for any pay for the clothes I bought him or for all the hours I spent trying to get him straightened out.'

"Though Dad was gone now, I could almost hear his earnest voice. 'Marc, a servant should be worthy of his hire, but he must decide in what coin he wants his pay.'

"I wondered if Dad ever knew the value of the gift he gave me on that hot summer day twenty years ago."

28 On His Right Hand

In the Savior's description of the final judgment he portrayed the determining factor in our final destiny — serving one another, giving the gift of love.

When the Son of man shall come in his glory, and all the holy angels with him, then shall he sit upon the throne of his glory:

And before him shall be gathered all nations: and he shall separate them one from another, as a shepherd divideth his sheep from the goats:

And he shall set the sheep on his right hand, but the goats on the left.

Then shall the King say unto them on his right hand, Come, ye blessed of my Father, inherit the kingdom prepared for you from the foundation of the world:

For I was an hungred, and ye gave me meat: I was thirsty, and ye gave me drink: I was a stranger, and ye took me in:

Naked, and ye clothed me: I was sick, and ye visited me: I was in prison, and ye came unto me.

Then shall the righteous answer him, saying, Lord, when saw we thee an hungred, and fed thee? or thirsty, and gave thee drink?

When saw we thee a stranger, and took thee in? or naked, and clothed thee?

Or when saw we thee sick, or in prison, and came unto thee?

And the King shall answer and say unto them, Verily I say unto you, Inasmuch as ye have done it unto one of the least of these my brethren, ye have done it unto me. (Matthew 25:31-40.)